THIS BOOK
BELONGS TO

....

....

Thank you for Purchasing my book and taking the time to read it from front to back. I am always grateful when a reader chooses my work and I hope you enjoyed it!

With the vast selection available online, I am touched that you chose to be purchasing my work and take valuable time out of your life to read it. My hope is that you feel you made the right decision.

I very much would like to know what you thought of the book. Please take the time to write an honest and informative review on Amazon.com. Your experience and opinions will be of great benefit to me and those readers looking to make an informed choice.

With much thanks.

@COPYRIGHT 2024

The content contained within this book may not be reproduced, duplicated, or transmitted without direct written permission from the author or the publisher. Under no circumstances will any blame or legal responsibility be held against the publisher, or author, for any damages, reparation, or monetary loss due to the information contained within this book. Either directly or indirectly.

Legal Notice:
This book is copyright protected. This book is only for personal use. You cannot amend, distribute, sell, use, quote, or paraphrase any part, or the content within this book, without the consent of the author or publisher.

Disclaimer Notice:
Please note the information contained within this document is for educational and entertainment purposes only. All effort has been executed to present accurate, up-to-date, and reliable, complete information. No warranties of any kind are declared or implied. Readers acknowledge that the author is not engaging in the rendering of legal, financial, medical, or professional advice. The content within this book has been derived from various sources. Please consult a licensed professional before attempting any techniques outlined in this book. By reading this document, the reader agrees that under no circumstances is the author responsible for any losses, direct or indirect, which are incurred as a result of the use of the information contained within this document, including, but not limited to — errors, omissions, or inaccuracies.

Table of Contents

Introduction	5
Chapter 1: Introduction to R Data Visualization	10
Chapter 2: Basic Plotting With ggplot2	25
Chapter 3: Advanced Visualization with ggplot2	38
Chapter 4: Statistical Analysis in Plotting and Scatterplots with ggstatsplot (gggo)	51
Chapter 5: Visualization and Model Interpretation	64
Chapter 6: External Libraries	76
Chapter 7: Self-Documenting Code	88
Chapter 8: Other R Packages for Data Visualization and Analysis	100
Conclusion	115

Introduction

Data visualization is the process of representing data graphically. Data visualization helps in the exploration and understanding of data. It is said to be more efficient and time-saving than other forms of data representation like tables or text lists. Data visualization can be used in almost all fields, including IT, science and engineering, finance, and business. It is also used in explaining complex data to people.

Data Visualization has become a part of our lives through the increasing number and variety of digital devices like computers and cellular phones. A single device such as a computer can display data in many ways: text, numeric values, image bitmaps, or graphic objects. Each data view gives a different perspective on the information captured in the dataset and can be used for specific purposes. A gallery of a group of data visualizations presents a set of images that show how the same dataset is displayed in different formats.

Data visualization serves as an efficient means of communication and to help understand, analyze, model, and process data. Visualizing data enables understanding its structure and allows making assumptions about it. However, it helps the users identify patterns in the data and aids them in making decisions based on the results. It is possible to communicate the data value and designs easily and quickly with the help of visual representations.

Visualization of data involves representing it understandably to a person or a machine. Visualizations are application-specific and generic. Application-specific visualizations are helpful only in specific applications, while generic visualizations can be used across several applications without any modification required. The data of any application domain is quantified by a set of semantics specific to the field.

Data visualization tools enable the rapid development of custom applications for communicating information and exploring business intelligence values. It also provides an effective way for social media users with no technical background to understand what is presented by visually analyzing the data.

Visualization processing is a crucial component of the visualization process that involves the design, development, and presentation of data visualizations. It encompasses the following steps: data acquisition, data transformation, metadata preparation, and scripting to create the desired visualizations.

Data visualization is not just translating information but also interpreting it in a meaningful way. It helps create a mental model by which we can interpret new information our eyes are giving us. This interpretation provides us with an understanding of numbers, facts, pictures, or any collection of data items that can be depicted using the most appropriate communication and visualization tool. Visualization methods are used to communicate in different ways that shape and organize the meaning to be understood easily and quickly without getting confused.

Data visualization has the power to transform the way we understand, interact, analyze and communicate data. When data is accessible to everyone, its value becomes immense. Visualization improves communication among people, builds an understanding between peers, and enhances collective knowledge. Visualization allows one to identify patterns in data quickly and process them without much effort. It also helps in conveying large amounts of information at one time through a single image or chart rather than long texts or lists of numbers.

Data visualization helps identify quantitative relationships, where it is easier to make inferences concerning underlying data, especially in large databases. The value of visualization lies in its ability to keep users focused on the essential aspects of the data and make them aware of critical patterns within the data set. Visualization lets us better comprehend abstract notions such as velocity and volume or compare human behavior with the patterns observed by environmental and social scientists. Visualization can be used to demonstrate a correlation between two variables or to show differences between several variables.

Visualization has been found to explain different types of real-world phenomena that may not necessarily be evident from their physical forms. It also aids in understanding relationships between data sets which may not be easily noticed or considered by people. Thus, it enables an effective way of showing various aspects of data through graphics, flow charts, and pictorial representations.

Visualization has become an essential component of today's computer world. It is a quick way to represent large amounts of complex information for better understanding. Visual representations are more effective in communicating information to people than text descriptions or numbers because they give users better clues about variations from the norm, trends, and anomalies. Visualization of information is also more effective than text descriptions which may lead to misinterpretation.

Visualization is not just a way to display data. Still, it is a technique to communicate the meaning that data represents, and it provides users with an understanding of the data's origin and its relationships with other data sets.

Visualization represents many different types of information, including performance indicators in businesses, social patterns in communities, and environmental or biological problems. It can also mean abstract notions such as financial trends, human behaviors, or management levels.

In general, everything that involves communicating information in images, graphs, text, and other graphic representations is visualization processing.

Data visualization converts data into an easily interpretable form that leads to better decisions, facilitate understanding of new knowledge, and widens business efficiency. Data visualization is a powerful communication tool for capturing, communicating, and visually presenting information. It helps in making decisions by visualizing data results. It also displays the progress made on a real-time basis within organizations. Visualization processing is a crucial step in the visualization process; it involves designing, developing, and presenting data visualizations.

Visualization processing encompasses the following steps: data acquisition, data transformation, metadata preparation, and scripting or custom-developed scripts to create desired visualizations tools.

Data visualization is done using three-dimensional techniques, including 3D surfaces, bar charts, pie charts, maps and scatter plots.

Visualization can be used for more than just displaying the data. It can be used to identify relationships among different variables. An excellent example of this is how medical researchers use visualization to identify patterns in genome sequences. Data visualization is heavily used in social sciences, allowing us to better understand the behaviors of populations. These are just several examples of the many areas where data visualization can be used.

Visualization is used for various purposes, including communication and presentation of data, information about unknown entities, demonstration and simulation of new ideas and possibilities in science, visual representation of mathematical formulas, visualization, and visualization processing to facilitate understanding and decision making.
Visualization can also communicate scientific research results by displaying experiments in graphical form.

In software, development visualization is essential because it helps programmers communicate with their customers.

Chapter 1: Introduction to R Data Visualization

Data visualization is one of the most powerful tools in a scientist's toolkit, but it is not always easy to build compelling visualizations with little or no previous experience. The hardest part of creating a visualization is deciding what data to visualize and how. The second most challenging part is finding the data. This book will teach you how to create effective, interactive displays from the basic building blocks of R data visualizations: plots, maps, and text. You will learn how to set up projects on your local computer, download data from websites, transform your files and manipulate them for visualization purposes before you can create visualizations with R.

In this book, you'll learn the basic building blocks of R data visualizations (plots, maps, and text) and how to use data to gather information before you can begin creating visualizations in R.

You will also learn to analyze continuous and categorical variables, merge multiple datasets into one file for analysis, create line charts with simple legend support for your plots, and create 3D graphs with numerous layers of data on a 2D field. Create highly flexible bar charts that easily support multi-variable or multi-line charting templates.

You can use these charts to create interactive visualizations online using D3 or high charts rather than the default R graph output.

By the end of this book, you will be able to create your own compelling data visualization projects from scratch in R and integrate them into existing websites and social media platforms with little or no technical experience.

If you are interested in statistics, data analysis, or the social sciences, R is probably on your radar already. This free software language is used to perform statistical analysis and data visualization and has a growing community of developers and users across various disciplines around the globe.

The R language was first developed in the early 1990s. The current version of the language is commonly referred to as R Core or R, and a stable version of it is distributed for free by a nonprofit organization known as the R Foundation for Statistical Computing.

The latest version is R 3.1.2, released on 7 July 2016. This article describes how to download and install the most recent R version.

R can be installed from CRAN, a large repository containing over 10 thousand contributed packages written by researchers, developers, and academics worldwide. To access CRAN, enter the following command in R:

Install.packages("package-name")

This will download and install the package on your computer.

If you haven't heard about R yet or are just getting started with it, one of the best ways to learn how it works is by exploring its built-in visualization capabilities using their shiny new d3 package.

The d3 package is a great companion to R because it makes it easy to create charts and maps in R but integrates them with the popular D3 JavaScript library for interactive client-side web applications.

The d3 methods that you'll learn in this book will make it easy for you to export your R visualizations into HTML/CSS, CSS Grid Frameworks such as Bootstrap, or even serve them directly from a server-side API using Node.js.

You can use these charts to create interactive visualizations online using D3 or high charts rather than the default R graph output.

This book is for anyone who wants to learn about the d3 package capabilities and how to work with them through various examples.

You'll learn how to create visualization charts in R and then integrate them with d3 code for client-side display in web applications and how to make your interactive web applications using R and d3.

This book is designed to follow the "R Programming: Packed with Data Visualization" book you will find here. However, it also can be used on its own.
The text begins by covering the basic theory of visualizing data and where computer science meets statistics. It will then cover basic R-based data visualization principles and examples of how to create effective, interactive displays from the start.

It will cover the basics of how to use d3 as integration with R's visualization capability and access it through a RESTful API.

The text replicates much of the material described herein in the free "R Programming: Packed with Data Visualization" book.

It also includes examples that you can run on your computer to learn how to integrate R and d3 seamlessly together. These examples will provide you with a foundation for creating your powerful visualizations in R and then incorporating them into your website or application.

The book focuses on the usability of interactive data visualization examples and builds upon your knowledge so that you can create your visualizations based on your specific data.

It teaches you how to use R, d3, and a variety of other techniques which take advantage of R's built-in visualization capability.

The book also includes a variety of tips, tricks, and shortcuts to increase your productivity and more advanced topics such as how to improve the quality of your graphic output.

The book is written for all levels of programmers, from novice to advanced. It assumes that you have experience with R and have a basic understanding of creating charts in R by using the base graphics engine.

You can also use these charts to create interactive visualizations online using D3 or high charts rather than the default R graph output. You can also use these charts to create interactive visualizations online using D3 or high charts instead of the default R graph output.

This book is written for all levels of programmers, from novice to advanced. It assumes that you have experience with R and have a basic understanding of creating charts in R by using the base graphics engine.

The text begins by covering the basic theory of visualizing data and where computer science meets statistics. It will then cover basic R-based data visualization principles and examples of how to create effective, interactive displays from the start.

What is R?

R is a language for statistical computing and graphics. It replaced the older S language (now called R classic). R provides various statistical and graphical techniques, including linear and nonlinear modeling, classical statistical tests, time-series analysis, classification, clustering, etc. The R language is widely used among statisticians and data miners for developing statistical software and data analysis. Because of its S heritage, R has better compatibility with applications developed in C/C++, Fortran, and Java.

At first glance, R seems to be a programming language to crunch numbers. R is exceptionally good at manipulating data. Developers write many packages (literally thousands) to tackle specific data manipulation problems. Even more impressive, the framework itself is free and open-source. Statisticians and other analysts worldwide use R to share and visualize their results.

What does the acronym "R" mean?

It's pronounced "aree." It stands for "the R Project for Statistical Computing." The term originated from a typo in the titles of papers written by John Chambers, inventor of the language, who had an accident with his keyboard and wrote 'RR' instead of 'RR.'

DataViz: Data Visualization With R

DataViz is an open-source java-based library that provides some of the most commonly used visualization tools using data frames created using the R programming language. It was built using Hibernate API to take advantage of all its advantages. This framework provides a wide range of visualizations like Histograms, Box Plots, Scatter Plots, Bar Charts, etc., which can be easily integrated into reports or exported to html pages or pdf as vectors images.

R is designed around an S programming language syntax. Unlike most earlier programming languages that use C style syntax, such as FORTRAN or C++, which require the programmer to allocate all their variables before using them, R permits the programmer to create new variables while they are in use. The R environment also provides graphics parameters to produce publication-quality graphs in either raster or vector formats (or both) without any external graphics software.

R can run on all popular operating systems, including Microsoft Windows, UNIX/Linux, and Mac OS. A companion project, called RStudio, provides a graphical user interface for R.

R is extremely popular with statisticians and data miners to develop statistical software and data analysis.

In January 2006, R became the most widely used programming

language in statistics, according to the TIOBE Programming Community Index. In May 2011, R was ranked third among programming languages in a survey of 7,500 developers by RedMonk. In June 2011, R came 3rd after Java and Python in a Stack Overflow user poll asking, "What do you use to analyze data."

The R Language was created in 1996 by Ross Ihaka and Robert Gentleman of the University of Auckland in New Zealand. It was designed to help them analyze ecological data sets with the aim that other researchers would find the language useful for their work. Ihaka and Gentleman made the source code available over the Internet so that others could contribute enhancements more easily than before. The popularity of R began to grow as it was adopted in other applications.

The R Foundation was established in 2004 to protect and maintain the R project, provide infrastructure for its ongoing development, and promote its use. And from the same year, R started a new versioning scheme which correlated with the year of release of a new feature into the language. So currently, there is version 3.1 (released in November 2014).

Today, R is used in many fields. It is often the programming language of choice outside other statistical languages such as SAS, SPSS, and Stata. The open-source community around R provides many libraries to complement the core language. These allow people to work with large data sets, create charts and maps, manipulate textual data and perform general numerical calculations.

What does this allow you to do?

One of the key features of R is its data visualization capabilities. Using R, you can create bubble charts, bar charts, histograms, density plots—pretty much anything your heart desires. The possibilities are almost endless! You can also set up graphs with multiple x-axes or y-axes to compare different quantitative variables in one plot.

Note: R plots are saved as gifs with a .png extension. This presents an issue when you move files to another computer or computer operating system, and R can't read the file. For example, if you save the chart with a different extension (e.g., .pdf) on your home computer, and then you want to copy that same chart to your school's server, it will not work because only gif files are supported by their server. Thus, all of your charts can be saved as gifs or pngs in this case.

R is also helpful for other purposes requiring complex graphics despite its statistical capabilities. For example, business analysts can create charts and graphs in R to track or summarize their data. The potential uses for graphing with R are virtually endless!

Another primary use of R is in compiler design, where a lot of R's statistics and graphics capabilities are used during the compilation process. This is why statistics and computing go hand-in-hand—they both rely heavily on visualizations to explain trends and patterns. Developing graphics capabilities in programming languages has been necessary since the beginning stages of visualization.

In summary, R excels at statistical computing and graphically analyzing information. Its capability as a tool for data analysis allows you to see trends or patterns that may be hidden with other statistical methods.

Why Learn Data Visualization with R?

Data visualization is a hot topic in data analysis and statistics. It enables you to turn your raw data into meaningful and easy-to-understand graphs, charts, and maps that are much more fun to look at than long lists of numbers. Data visualization is all about creating the illusion of the data in many ways, but one of the most popular is with graphs and charts.

But why is this important? Imagine you just took a survey of all the people in your state, and you've got all their answers. But where to begin? It is just a bunch of numbers, and it doesn't make as much sense as possible. You need to do something with the data to make sense of it. You can visualize it to see patterns or use it to answer existing questions.

Two essential steps in developing a good visualization are data cleaning and selection. You want your data to be as close to perfect as possible. Any bad points should be corrected before applying any other technique. If you have incorrect or misleading data, there will be no way for your visualization to tell you what you need to know about the outcome.

A clean data set is essential for creating a good representation of numerical information. This can be done through the process of data transformation. Data transformation plays a vital role in the analysis. It provides a means to fit calculations to specific problems and helps to solve the problem. In the case of this visualization, it has been used to determine specific areas that need improving and what is going well.

Data visualization is also growing more vital because we find that information presented in different media affects our ability to remember it differently. So depending on what kind of presentation you want your audience to have, you would use different types of data visualizations for the same data set.

R can store all your data for later use, allowing easy manipulation and revision if desired. This is important for you to see if your data is accurate before publishing. If you are using Excel, there is always a chance that something has changed on the computer without you knowing.

R also has compelling graphics capabilities. It's easy to learn, making it easier to create good visualizations with less effort. As you become more comfortable working with data visualization in R, you'll find that many more tasks of this nature are straightforward in R than in other programs.

Finally, R supports data visualization tools that no other program does. With the use of various tools, you can construct fantastic visualizations quickly and easily. You can even combine multiple devices, creating incredibly complex and exciting visualizations.

The best way to learn data visualization is through practice. This means that you will have to do your own data visualization repeatedly as you know to do it correctly. Before long, you will find that these tasks become easy to accomplish and will become a lot of fun!

Another reason to learn data visualization with R and not another software program is that many other benefits come with doing so. The most important of these benefits is creating interactive visualizations (such as maps) and static graphs (such as bar charts). If you want a static graph, you can easily make it in Excel. But if you wish for interactive visualizations, these are a lot harder to create in Excel. On the other hand, R will allow you to do this without problems.

You can also use R to create static plots containing your data and no axes or titles (all the data visualization elements are visible but not interactive). These static plots are very useful for presentations. You can make them in PowerPoint too, but then they would be static images rather than actual charts (this will make turning them into accurate Charts much more difficult). R also allows you to have interactive visualizations that contain both data and interactivity. Of course, the more complex the visualization, the more difficult it may be. However, R has a lot of functionality to help make things easier.

When your data visualization is finished, you can save it as an image and then share it with your colleagues or publish it on the Internet. Thanks to its open-source nature, r will allow you as many people as possible to see and use your visualizations. You can also embed these images in blogs or other online platforms for a large audience to use.

Who is This Book For?

This book has the idea of helping someone new to data science get started and make their first visualizations. This includes people who are currently interested in data gathering but have not yet decided on what they want to pursue and the people who know they want a career in data science but do not know where to start.

The book is designed for people who have a basic understanding of Python and a knowledge of statistics. The book focuses on data science but can also be used to introduce programming in general. It does not assume you have any experience with Python, but you should have at least a working knowledge of Python. The book does not think you have any experience with data science. However, it does assume you have some experience with statistics and can understand basic statistical formulas.

The book is an excellent introduction to data visualization in R. Although the book and many of the visuals use R, it can be applied to other languages that use R as an interface, such as Shiny.

This book is not a comprehensive tutorial on data science and should be read alongside other resources. This book is not a reference or textbook and does not give you the final answer on everything you need to do to make your first data visualizations. All technical details of the visuals are available in the R code and online resources, so this book should be used as more of a jumping-off point than an all-in-one resource.

Why This Is An Incredible Book for Beginners?

This book is written in a way that anyone who reads it can use what they have learned to see if they want to pursue learning data science further or not. In other words, this book takes you from the beginning of why you want to get into data science and what the world of data science is.

This book considers that it is a beginner's book and has less focus on mathematical details like statistics. Readers will learn what kinds of functions are available in R. Still; it will not go over every parameter trick or formula used to create different visuals. The math section is still included but has been made more accessible without getting bogged down in specific procedures or too much detail on programming.

Suppose you are interested in becoming a data scientist. In that case, this book will explain how to analyze data and design visualizations that may be used as part of your purposeful research. This book was written for people who wanted to be able to implement data visualization within their projects but were not sure where to start. With this in mind, you may decide that you are interested in a career in data science. In this case, you will learn some of the basics about how our brains react to visual information and how we can harness the power of design principles to help get your message across. This book is also meant for people curious about the world around them and who want to learn more by collecting and analyzing vast amounts of data and then creating visuals that tell a story.

In short, this book will give you the tools necessary to use visualizations (i.e., graphs and charts) to get you more information about your data. This can help you gain perspective on what's going on with it to make more informed decisions.

What Will I Learn from This Book?

R is a software for statistical computing and data manipulation, based on the language of "The Jagged Array" (which is a data structure in computer science). People need this software for their analysis.

This book will walk you through generating projections of your data so you can get what R has to offer with ease. It goes over how to use R's base and lattice graphics functions and its functions, including ggplot2, which is an alternative package that comes with many high-quality visualizations ready to go out of the box. This goes beyond simple graphs, but it also covers back-end and front-end introduction using Python or Matlab/Octave.

The book assumes a good working knowledge of other programming languages, such as C++ and Java. There is a lot of code in this book, so it is assumed that you have at least some working proficiency with R and that you are comfortable and familiar with using R's essential functions and its graphical functions.

This book is intended to help the reader gain greater insight and practical experience with visualization packages in R. You will need some knowledge of R programming. This is a book, but it has additional resources to supplement it. If you do not know how to use R, please learn it and then return to this book.

Why Visualize Data?

Visualizing data is an effective way of understanding what is going on with data, whether the structure or some event or issue. After all, visuals are compelling in turning abstract numbers into something we can see!

First Things First — Installation and SetupAt this stage, you should have a working package installation of R on your computer and a working knowledge of the basic features, functions, and graphical capabilities of R's base graphics system.

There are several ways to install and set up R, so it is crucial to choose the right one: Install R using your operating system's package manager. R is available as part of many different applications and software packages. For example, use your preferred installer for MySQL or Postgresql if you want to add R as a dependency within an installer.

Install R from the source if you can. You can download the latest source code from the project page, compile it from the start, and install it on your computer. This is the best way to learn how R works daily.

Install R as a gem. R is also available as a gem, and you will install it on your computer by using your preferred gem manager. If you are new to Ruby Gems, this is the best way to start learning about them and how to use them with R.

Install R using the CRAN package repository. The CRAN package repository is an official repository for many software packages, including popular ones like R. You know, have fewer dependencies and fewer road-blocks when installing packages in this way.

Installing R using the CRAN repository is simple. Visit the project page and choose to install R in your package manager of choice. One thing to be aware of, though, if using the CRAN package repository, is that packages cannot be installed at specific R versions, or they will not work automatically.

This guide was written specifically for operating systems such as Linux, and Mac OS X. Windows users should install R using the CRAN package repository on Windows.

Installing Packages from the CRAN Repository

The process for installing different packages from the CRAN package repository is relatively simple. For example, if you want to install ggplot2, the process would be:

Install ggplot2 using the R command script. Execute this command in R: > install. Packages ('ggplot2') The command-line interface to R will now finish installing ggplot2. To verify that the package was installed correctly, use the R command: > vignette("ggplot2"). This will display a list of commands you can use with ggplot2. These are the recommended commands for using ggplot2. If you see the message below, your installation went well: Kernel is in the 'main' folder /usr/lib/R/library. The rest of your installation should go smoothly.

First Steps in Base Graphics

R's base graphics system is the default graphical interface for R. It allows you to create straightforward, static plots and very flexible plots customized to your own specific needs and taste.

The following examples will show you how to create some basic plots from scratch. Later, we will cover how to use the different packages that come with R so you can get them up and running without too much hassle.

The Basics of the Plot FunctionA line plot is a great way to visualize data points over time, either by date or value: a line plot connects points based on their weight.

The plot function can take various parameters. The simplest way to do this is to specify the parameters by name, with =. For example, a simple line plot of your data would be:

➢ # Use > # x = c(1, 2, 3) > # y = c(4, 5, 6) > plot(x=x, y=y) This will create a simple line plot that simply connects each point between them in your dataset. To change the appearance of the line type and other visual elements, you'll need to use different functions built into base graphics.

Start by looking at the main plot functions. There are many different plot types you can select from, and these can be used to customize how your line plots look.

Chapter 2: Basic Plotting With ggplot2

Ggplot is a system for declaratively creating graphics based on The Grammar of Graphics. To create a plot:

1) Specify the data to be shown in the graphic, which may be a table, histogram, or some other type of frequency distribution;

2) Decide on one or more variables that should be summarized (e.g., "height" might translate "gender") and indicate their $function$ as geom_bar(), geom_histogram(), etc.

To create a basic plot, we will first create a ggplot object, which contains your data, and from that, a layer of graphics options. We can then add gem layers (which draw in different ways with different aesthetics) to make the plot we like. Note that you can also specify multiple layers of gems at one time by adding them to the layers list. For example geom_histogram() + stat_bin() is equivalent to I+geom_histogram(binwidth=stat_bin()) which you will see below

Note that you can use any function as an aesthetic, so it is easy to change these plots using other functions instead e.g.

Ggplot2 is a system for creating graphics based on "The Grammar of Graphics." It implements a particular data visualization approach geared towards exploratory and analytical data analysis. Ggplot2 is inspired by Leland Wilkinson's grammar of graphics but has been rewritten from scratch, adding new functionality and making several improvements.

The syntax for creating and modifying graphs in R is based on the grammar structure. A plot is a single object, and the data to be used is specified by the main argument. The main idea may accept several data types, which are then used to create other graphics.

The Grammar of Graphics

The Grammar of Graphics is a system for conceptualizing data visualization. It starts from the basic principle of grammar and then provides an approach for visualizing data.

The Grammar of Graphics attempts to create a systematic way to understand and communicate data by using visuals. The goal is not to make plots attractive but rather to create understandable representations of the data you are working with. This system can be followed for any data visualization. It starts with a given graph representing the key concepts in your dataset, but it also has the plotting functions that allow you to tweak this plot in many different ways and extends it into new areas that fit with your knowledge base.

Plotting functions in ggplot2 require two things, namely, a data frame and a geometrical object to map that data frame onto. It would help if you had a dataset (or "dataframe") and the coordinates of one or more points on the screen or page that don't touch each other. There are a few ways to get the data into R. As with any software; you can read data directly from files (and many formats are supported) or bring it into R using a function that saves it as text in an R variable. Some raw statistical data can be obtained directly into R with the use of specialized functions. Some packages download data for you, though this is primarily useful if the dataset is not public and you want to clean your code.

Different geometrical objects can represent the same data in different ways. The two most important ones are points (geom_point) and lines (geom_line). Both geom types are beneficial for plotting, but lines are more suited to describing the characteristics of a population. The coordinates and the graph type (points or lines) are entirely interdependent and should be kept in sync.

Three main geometrical objects can be mapped onto the data:

points, lines, and polygons.

Points (geom_point) map numerical data onto an x-y coordinate plane. They indicate the central point of a group of observations. This group is defined by its center; when a point is added to a graph and plotted, it draws a circle with its center. These circles can have different radii depending on your dataset's x- and y-values. A point can have x and y coordinates or an entire continuous axis.

Lines (geom_line) are used to create histograms with lines of different widths according to the data, rather than using the discrete points used for geom_point. Generally, a line should be better suited for representing continuous data than a point. Still, there are cases where an issue is preferable because it preserves variation in the data. Lines can also be plotted on top of points, but any numerical information about the dataset invalid as it will not show up unless you force it.

A point can be plotted on a line (geom_smooth), representing a continuous variable. It is helpful to indicate that the dataset is continuous, but it does not give any additional information about what the variable looks like.

Polygons (geom_polygon) are for mapping categorical variables onto an axis where x and y coordinates are used to define multiple regions. They can be used as a histogram because they show how many observations fall into each category.

Polygons are particularly easy to use with string variables because you can define the names of the categories as strings instead of numbers or other data types. They are also helpful when you want to add text to your plots.

Geom_polygon extends the introductory geom_polygon class that allows specifying different categories for each value. The attributes fill, color, and show are always the same as a regular polygon. One crucial difference is that if more than one category per value, you can set min and max expressivity by using them and min attributes, respectively. The expand attribute (the default) will make your polygons almost as much like points as possible, with particular attention to separating them in case of large categorical values. The alpha attribute controls transparency.

The next step is to map this geometrical object onto the data, which is done by defining the x and y coordinates of a geom_line or geom_point. In ggplot2, there is a little more to it because you need to decide whether the x-axis should be mapped as "x" or "x." These are called facets in ggplot2, and they are what allow you to define different variables for each axis. There are many ways to use facets, and it's essential to understand how they work. One way is to map all the points to one x-axis and choose the corresponding y-coordinates as they come along. This allows you to map a single variable, like total sales, onto one axis.

Another example is mapping two variables onto both axes and choosing nonlinear relationships between them. You need to select a mapping function that tells ggplot2 how one variable is related to another. There are many different functions for this, but the most commonly used one is bin2rgb() which constructs a continuous variable from three categorical variables by assigning values based on their position in a string of categories. Naturally, you can use more than three variables and map them onto more than two axes. This function is handy for coloring the polygons in a thematic map.

The last thing you need to do is tell ggplot2 how you want to display all of this on your screen or page. You do this by defining the title and axis labels using labs() and the x and y scales using xlab() and lab().

You can also specify what happens at the edges of your graph. The geom_polygon object has a 'boundary' option that can be used to draw lines around your polygons. The width of these lines can be controlled by the bandwidth and shape attributes.

Pruning is removing outliers (extreme values) from a dataset. Outliers are values that stray from the center of an observed distribution; technically speaking, outliers are extreme values in an iteratively estimated density plot (i.e. outlying data points). Pruning removes this data and allows for improved statistical analysis.

Many data visualization libraries have outlier control functions; however, they often involve cutting points from the original dataset. Tibble also now has an outlier package to deal with outliers. This is an excellent example of how outlier removal can be handled differently between different software packages.

The table library has an outlying function that cuts a column of data based on its median value.

Poisson regression is a popular way to find county-level relationships in time-series databases such as log files and payment transactions. A Poisson distribution is a probability distribution used in modeling and analyzing the number of events per unit of time. The Poisson model can estimate the expected count in a given time interval based on the mean number per unit of time.

The function prcomp() can be used to detect any suspicious outliers that are present in the data. This function is commonly used in R to check variables for heteroscedasticity (variable variance) as it returns an object of the class that stores variance inflation factors (VIF) values. If there are too many outliers, their variance might inflate the actual conflict; this could mean something wrong with your data or model.

Tibble is a package for converting the output from saving functions such as dplyr into dataframes. The goal of this is to help in visualizing and understanding the data. The outlying package can be used to detect natural and artificial outliers; it uses functions from the purrr, visdev, and tidyr packages, so there will be no need to install any extra boxes. The outlier function creates a geom_point object and a series of labels that follow the format 'x, y'. This means that to use this package, you must already have a way of dealing with points in R. To do this, you will need to have specific packages installed, such as ggplot2.

Tidygraph is a network package for R that provides interactive graph exploration and visualization tools. The function tidygraph_prune can be applied to remove artifacts from a network and will remove vertices (nodes) that contain only duplicate edges. This function can be used for eliminating artificial outliers; however, this is not its primary purpose.

If you want to visualize the difference between the original and pruned graph, you could use the helper function from_df() to convert the network object into a dataframe. This will allow you to plot your graph using points, lines, or shapes.

Basic Plots

Ggplot2 is a powerful plotting system for R (often called the "Swiss Army Knife of graphics") that can be used to create static plots, interactive web graphics, LaTeX plots and more.

Ggplot2 passes data from the plot function to other functions for style and theme. It uses geometry objects to represent graphical primitives in order to compute layouts such as position adjustments.

In this article we will go from generating a basic scatter plot through adding some additional elements and styling it with ggplot2.

Scatter Plot

The ggplot2 scatter plot is particularly useful for illustrating relationships between two variables.

Example: Basic Scatter Plot

```
Library(ggplot2)
Require(MASS)
Attach(mtcars)
P <- ggplot(data=mtcars, aes(x=wt, y=mpg)) + geom_point() + stat_smooth()
P + coord_cartesian(xlim=c(-3,3), ylim=c(-1.5,2.5))
P + geom_point(aes(color= factor(cyl))) + fte_theme()
P + geom_point(aes(color= factor(cyl))) + ggthemes::scale_color_brewer()
```

Changing Line Styles, Colors and Size

The line elements in ggplot2 are implemented using the geom_line() function. There are three arguments for this function: geometry, aes and size. The geometry argument controls the type of line to plot: straight, dotted, dashed etc. The aes argument controls how the second variable is mapped to the y-axis – the default mapping is linear. Finally, the size argument controls the line thickness.

In addition to basic plotting with geom_line(), thicker lines can be created with aes(size=.5) and diverging lines can be created with aes(size=-1).

Since the size argument controls the line thickness, we can change the line thickness by adding more spaces between line elements.

Adding a Text Label

Since our data set includes both numeric and textual variables, there are several ways to specify an appropriate label in a ggplot2 plot. The geom_text() function allows us to specify text to be plotted in the same place as aes objects. This is done by specifying strings as values for names that take on the default format of "factor(cyl)".

For example,

P + geom_text(data=diamonds, aes(color=cut), label="Cut") + labs(x="Carat", y="Price")

Clearly we do not want our text to come below the data points and we might not even want the text to be visible. Therefore the geom_text() function takes an additional argument indicating whether or not to indicate a position for the text. If you don't include an argument it will be placed where the aes objects are normally placed.

The labs() function can be used to add axis titles and labels. One thing to note here is how spacing matters when labeling your axes. The value labs(x="...") is a label for the x-axis. The value below that is the label of the y-axis.

Finally, it is common to use a left margin in text labels and to center the text in the plot area. This can be achieved by using coord_flip() to flip over your axes, adding extra space to the right and directing text to be centered between coordinate tick marks using theme().

P + geom_text(data=diamonds, aes(color=cut), label="Cut") + labs(x="Carat", y="Price", title="Diamond Carat And Price Chart") + theme(axis.title.x=element_text(size=14), axis.text.x = element_text(vjust=-0.5)) + theme(plot.title = element_text(hjust=0, vjust=-0.2))

The ggplot package aims to make it easy to create high-quality graphics in R by taking care of many of the "plumbing" details that other packages require you to handle yourself (e.g., producing legends and correctly labeling axes).

Basic Plotting with svydesign and svly()

Data visualization is an important part of assessing the insights in data. The ability to visualize data is a skill that improves with experience, and well executed plots can be a vital part of the compelling analysis. In this post, I provide three common plots that are sometimes referred to as 'Beyond the basics'.

The first plot is called a cumulative frequency graph and looks similar to a histogram, but it only tabulates the frequency over smaller intervals rather than aggregating them all together. This approach can be useful for quickly assessing trends across variables where large differences appear more frequently at lower frequencies (i.e., less prevalent) than at higher frequencies (i.e., more prevalent).

The second plot is called a quantile-quantile (Q-Q) plot. This compares the ordering of raw data values with corresponding values from a theoretical distribution. This is a useful method for quickly diagnosing if data follow a specified distribution (e.g., normal), although care is required when interpreting the results because Q-Q plots are sensitive to non-normality and can therefore be misleading.

The final plot shows some aspects of the central limit theorem, including how as the sample size increases, the distribution transforms into a normal distribution and also how that transform works as we increase the range of values being examined.

Sevydesign has a range of plots that can incorporate these basic plots to give a more accurate and complete overview of the data:

Plotting with svydesign Svly() and y2t() can also be used to create k-means clustering, which is useful for comparing different models of clustering. The following example shows how we can compare two models using the cluster sum of squares statistic.

Installing and using sevydesign The package can be installed from CRAN: install.packages("sevydesign")

getSvyDesign() provides a general overview of sevydesign. There are also vignettes that describe specific functions, such as getting started, plotting multiple variables this includes some examples of svly(), ggplot2() and qqmath(), and a companion document.

Svly() also has a companion document that describes the design and implementation.

Additionally, there is an R markdown vignette that describes using svydesign to create interactive web applications.

The principles of sevydesign

Sevydesign applies the principles of quality software development. It is a cleanly written, well documented R package that has full automated unit tests and utilises best practices such as test-driven development.

Seventy percent of the code for sevydesign is dedicated to quality assurance, including unit tests and validation of examples.

Svly(), an S3 generic function in sevydesign, provides a common API to all of the described plotting functions. An important benefit of this is that all aspects can be tested in one location rather than separately.

The sevydesign API is designed to be used with alternative plotting packages, not only base R graphics functions such as plot(). This makes it easy to make sevydesign calls transparently within other plotting packages. For example, using the dygraphs library and a call to the function trelliscope() is made easy when using svly().

The following example shows how to create a trelliscope plot that looks at the relationship between two variables: z <- ts (c (1 : 10, rnorm (10)), frequency = 12) svly (table (z))

Svly() attributes The various functions that allow the user to create plots have similar arguments. In order to make it easier to remember the arguments, svly() and other functions have an attribute 'attrs'. This allows the user to only specify the arguments that are different. For example:

Svly (table (z), yvar = "z", xvar = "x", data_frame = TRUE) This might be easier for beginning users than having to remember all of the arguments for all plotting functions.

This feature is not documented but can be viewed using: attr(,"attrs")

Extending sevydesign It would be possible to make sevydesign entirely from scratch, but it could result in inconsistencies or missing features. One advantage of using the package is that base R graphics work seamlessly with svly(), including features such as axes labels, title, facets, etc. Using svly() means that it should be easy to make all of these arguments easily accessible in any new plotting function added to sevydesign.

Using a third-party package might also save time when implementing new functionality, but it also has drawbacks. For example:

Extrapolation and interpolation These functions can be used to create simple extrapolations and interpolations between supplied values. This means that it is possible to turn any sevydesign function call into an options list for R Graphics.

Svly() will automatically apply any svly(attrs, value) type functions if it is known to be a valid value of the 'attrs' attribute. This means that packages such as ggplot2() can be used with ease, making cross-package calls in sevydesign easy and intuitive (e.g., calling a plot with svly(y) will adjust the legend labels). Another advantage is that all functions are tested for validity in all package environments. This means it cannot be accidentally passed invalid arguments that would otherwise behave in unexpected ways (e.g. axes in base R).

Svly() Svly() is an S3 generic function that provides a unified API across all functions in sevydesign. The following generic arguments are available:

'data_frame', 'table', 'factor', 'vector' (default=TRUE), 'position' (default=c(0.5,0)), and 'format_function' (default=quote(as.character)), which will be callable with input data arguments within the format specified by the plot. The most important argument is the plot type (e.g. 'plot'), as this specifies what plot type is being drawn and thus the main function being called. The default arguments are: 'plot', 'boxplot', 'lm' (linear model), 'histogram', and 'explanation' for an example of the general argument structure. In addition to the general function arguments, there are a number of special types of data that can be passed through to the functions (e.g. character), and these will be callable with their specified input argument name as stored in the svly() attribute data_frame. For example:

The "data" and "plot" arguments are also available in attributed form on both the function call (e.g. table(z, data_frame=TRUE)) and in the format string (e.g. xvar="data"). As explained above, svly() can be called with a bare data frame as a function argument but will return a data frame that has been extracted from the input object.

Svly() also has an attribute 'attrs' that can be used to specify additional arguments of svly(), such as colour palettes, etc. Since these arguments are specific to each plot type, they are not included in the general 'plot' argument, instead being specified using the same interface as for traditional R plotting functions. This allows the user to specify svly() arguments in an intuitive way by specifying the arguments that are different from those specified for other functions. Svyl() also has an attribute 'extras' which is a list of extra arguments to be passed on to the main plot function

Svly_colors() This function provides a set of colour palettes for use with svly(). The palettes were created using Adobe Kuler, an application that allows users to create colour themes. The following palettes are available:

(1) a set of bright and colourful themes;
(2) a set of themes based on data from RColorBrewer; and
(3) based on Hcl colours.

Svly_scales() This function provides a set of colour scales for use with svly(). These were created using Adobe Kuler, an application that allows users to create colour themes.

Chapter 3: Advanced Visualization with ggplot2

Whether you're analyzing data or making a product design, visualization is an important part of the process. With ggplot2 it's easy to make compelling graphs and plots with just a few lines of code.

Ggplot2 is an implementation of The Grammar of Graphics, an R visualization framework for designing graphics based on data. It's designed to be easy to use, not require specialized knowledge about graphics, and make the most effective use of your data. While it may seem like a strange statement, I believe that ggplot2 is the best way to visualize data in R.

Ggplot2 takes some of the tedium out of data visualization. For example, ggplot2 is able to automatically handle very complex data sets, such as networks and high-dimensional datasets. This makes it particularly useful for artists and designers who need to visualize very large or complex data sets. Other features include color palettes optimized for aesthetic appeal, a flexible and intuitive approach to layout design that fits any dataset, and a verbose and flexible API that allows you to draw the plot in any way you want—even if you have never used graphics programming before.

R Data visualization will teach you how to visualize data with ggplot2 in R. This is the most advanced and powerful way of visualizing data available in R: it is a revolution in data analysis.

What makes it so powerful? Here are some of its features: two-way interactions, hierarchical clustering, univariate and multivariate statistics. You will learn how to read and acquire data, use advanced statistical techniques, create publication quality graphics, and how to automate your analysis. You may be an intermediate R user and want to get started with ggplot2. Or you might be looking around for a book on R graphics that takes into account all the new features in ggplot2.

In this book you will learn how to use ggplot2 in a wide range of situations, from basic statistics and data exploration, to higher-level concepts like two-way interactions and visualizations. You will also learn how to automate your analysis using the new R packages: R Explore Cluster and R Package Installer. Finally, you will review the basics so that you can use ggplot2 in your own data visualization projects. This is not a comprehensive tutorial on ggplot2. It is aimed at advanced users who want to gain a deeper understanding of the principles behind ggplot2.

Ggplot2 was created by Hadley Wickham, who is one of the most prominent contributors to R software. He is also a fellow RStudio employee and an active member of the R community. The primary goal of the course is to create publication quality graphics. To this end, you will learn how to read and acquire data, use advanced statistical techniques and create publication-quality graphics with ggplot2.

You may be an intermediate R user and want to get started with ggplot2. Or you might be looking around for a book on R graphics that takes into account all the new features in ggplot2. In this course you will learn how to use ggplot2 in a wide range of situations, from basic statistics and data exploration, to higher-level concepts like two-way interactions and visualizations.

You will also learn how to automate your analysis using the new R packages: R Explore Cluster and R Package Installer. Finally, you will review the basics so that you can use ggplot2 in your own data visualization projects.

What is ggplot?

Ggplot is a graphics system based on the grammar of graphics. It is a powerful and expressive general-purpose graphic system for R. It allows you to draw graphical objects based on data, and then collect, summarize, and visualize that data in novel ways. To this end, it features flexible layout and styling, flexible axis specifications, efficient graphics device management, a variety of statistical functions for plotting graphs, automatic regression diagnostics for experimental design with multiple variables, many default visualization conventions, a powerful API for customizing the plot; and more.

Ggplot2 is developed and supported by members of the R Core Team, including Hadley Wickham, Romain Francois, and other members of the R community. The development of ggplot2 is sponsored by RStudio. Ggplot2 started as a rewrite of a plotting system called "The Grammar of Graphics" and much work on ggplot2 was inspired by Wilkinson's ideas.

The ggplot2 website includes a number of articles about ggplot, in addition to many examples for working with the system. While ggplot is developed by members of the R community, it is not affiliated with either R Foundation or The R Journal.

The system consists of two major components: a data visualization grammar in the form of a set of ggplot2 functions and associated data, and a base graphics layer (which is achieved by including codice_4 in the call to codice_5).

The layer specification framework is used to specify how layers are drawn. In this framework, layers are drawn via calls to the layer function. This function takes two arguments: an object that will be displayed on the plot (a "layer"), and an object describing how it should be drawn (the "data" argument). In most cases, a plot is drawn by calling codice_5 once for each layer that should be drawn.

The representation of data in ggplot2 is based on the idea of being able to represent "data objects". Each data object belongs to one and only one "dataset", and corresponds to some source of data (e.g., a vector named "data"). Data itself is represented by a list or array of objects. When plotted, data objects are drawn into a layer (e.g., the "graphics" layer) to form the plot.

Two layers are built into ggplot2: the "data" layer and the "aes" layer. The data layer contains a list of data objects that will be displayed by ggplot, while the aes layer contains all aesthetic mappings that describe how these data items should be drawn.

The output of the setup is an object; typically this is called "gg". To actually draw the plot, call one of the plotting functions: codice_5 or codice_7.

Typically, a data object will have one row of data and one column, so ggplot2 automatically treats the main axis as the forces (e.g., all other objects are placed on this axis). The code "gd" is used to draw a single (zero-dimensional) force. If you want to plot multiple forces, then use "gg". This function will ask you to specify two arguments: the second argument will be added as an additional layer for each additional force in your resulting plot. Specifying "codice_8" as the first argument is a special case that allows you to create a plot with only one force.

To add points, lines, or smooth curves, use the following functions: codice_9 (for points), codice_10 (for lines), and codice_11 (for smooth curves). The "data" object contains the data for each of these elements. If you want to overlay multiple lines or points on top of each other, then use an array of data objects instead; these functions will simply draw more than one line/point.

Faceting the Data

Facets are used to graph multiple related variables simultaneously (e.g., income by job type) or inspect subsets of the data that share a specific characteristic (e.g., males versus females). However, Faceting is also helpful in exploring the content of your data (e.g., the number of hits and number of males, or the number of males of a certain age).

When you use ggplot2, you can use Faceting to sample data from a range of values or explore which items appear in your dataset.

Ggplot2 allows facet_grid() or facet_grid(~x) to extract data from an entire range, or separate the portion by x. Since facetting pulls a subset out of your dataset, it's important to notice when you use "> it versus when you're not. Let's compare the syntax for a simple scatter plot with a faceted scatter plot.

In this example, we have a dataset with information about 2,000 earthquakes: location, magnitude, and time of occurrence. Let's create a simple scatterplot to explore the data.

Now let's add the facet_grid() function to explore how many earthquakes occur at different magnitudes and time intervals. This will allow us to filter out some of the noise and identify clustering in the data.

Since we are exploring earthquake magnitudes (x-axis), we should set facets along the x parameter using x ~ facets(~magnitude).

Now, let's check out how many earthquakes occur at higher magnitudes and different time intervals. Since we only want to see if there is any apparent clustering of higher magnitudes in short intervals of time, we will want a faceted scatterplot that only shows these portions. This will allow us to focus on the essential data.

In this example, the facet_grid() function takes in three parameters: x ~ facets(~magnitude | ~time) and gives us a scatterplot of earthquake magnitudes by time. There is some noticeable clustering in the data, and we can filter out any noise by using facets_on() in the ggplot() function. We can use this facet_grid() to find other exciting aspects of the data, like how long earthquakes take to occur or how long it takes for them to reach magnitude 6.

Inequalities of the scatterplot

You can use a facet_grid() function combined with facets_on() to see some of the relationships between the magnitudes, time, and location. You may notice that you create a faceted scatterplot and then immediately filter it by time. For example, this could explore other aspects of the data related to timing or any relationship between magnitudes over time.

To test this idea, I would create a simple scatterplot of earthquakes at different times by earthquake magnitude (magnitude ~ years since 1857) and filter for years more fabulous than 1800. Once this plot is created, I will use facets_on() to only show the results of magnitudes greater than six and years less than 2000. As a result, we are left with a graph showing us only earthquakes with magnitudes above six.

We need to modify our first scatterplot to include only magnitudes greater than 6. We will create a variable magnitude_flag, which will assign "True" if the magnitude is greater than or equal to 6 and "False" otherwise.

The faceted scatterplot consists of two functions: ggplot() and facet_grid(). ggplot() takes in a viewport and a list of x and facet values. The value of the first x will be used as the data for the plot, and the value of the second is used as a varying parameter to place facets along.

Ggplot() will take in all of these pieces, add them together, and plot this data in a scatterplot. In order to create this graph, use: ggplot(iris, aes(x=Sepal.Length)) + geom_point().

We assign Sepal. Length as our y-axis (variable), creating a scatterplot with 2 x 2 variance on the y-axis (variables). We also define Sepal—length as our aesthetic, or the variable that determines how to plot the data in our graph. The aesthetic of Sepal will define our x-axis width.

We then need to define focal_points and shape_args. We will use shape_args because we plot points on both axes (whereas focal_points would be used instead if we were using a histogram or density plot, focal_points would be used instead). We need to define an x and y variable for each axis. This can just be assigned as the same variable for each axis, which is then multiplied by a constant of 100: shape_args(x = c(0,.5,.5), y = c(0,.5,.5)). The x variable is the variable that is used in our plot, and the y variable is the variable that determines how many points are plotted on each axis.

We complete this graph by creating a few aesthetic parameters to annotate our plot. To annotate our plot, we will use standard functions like bar(), add_line(), and add_text() : bar(x = c(0,.5,.5) + digits(4), y = c(0,.5,.5) + digits(4))+ facet_grid(~factor ~ Year, ~magnitude | ~time) + labs(x="Seventeen-Year-Olds", y="Magnitude").

We use labs() to name our axes and pch and cex to annotate our points. In order to get the next graph, we will need to use facet_grid() with facets_on(). This function is similar to facet_grid(), but instead of creating a single plot with all facets, it creates multiple plots with different facets. For example, if you have a scatterplot with several x-axes, this function would create a separate scatterplot for each x variable.

We will use facets_on() to create the following graph. We set it up slightly differently, isolating the variables we are interested in and only showing them if they are True. This is done by adding AND as a suffix (in this case, ~magnitude>=6 AND ~time>=1800).

We then facet_grid() with facets_on(). The first argument is the data you want to filter for, factor(Year). We will be creating several plots for each year, so this can be considered the x-axis.

The second argument is what you want to filter for: magnitude > 6 or time > 1800.

The third argument is what you want to filter by magnitude or time.

Facet_grid() will create several plots. In the ggplot2 package, a function called facet_grid() can create these facets. If you want another plot with the same size, shape, and other parameters, use facet_grid() again.

At this point, we have created two different graphs for each of our x-axes, and each of these can be used to find other insights into the data.

If we want to compare earthquakes at different times across earthquake magnitudes, we can use a factor variable mask. This variable will only be used for one variable (in this case, magnitude).

We can use hclust() to visualize the data. We will use the hclust() function to find a hierarchical cluster representing the data best. For example, is it clear that earthquakes at magnitude six are clustered together, and earthquakes at magnitude 5-7 are spread apart among other clusters?

Hierarchical clustering

Hierarchical clustering is a type of data visualization where we visualize relationships between different variables or clusters of data. The idea is that each variable in our dataset can be broken down into different clusters based on their correlation with other variables and how they behave in a dimensional space (like distance on a map).

We can visualize the data using the dist() function, which determines the distance between variables.

To test this out, we will use a similar scatterplot as before, but this time with earthquake magnitudes and magnitude-time pairs.

We will need to calculate the correlation between each variable and every other variable. The first step is to map our data into a 2d space by using coord_map(). This will make it easier for us when we start summing up squares in our graphs. We show that we have each variable mapped into 2d space by assigning x = c(0,.5,.5) and y = c(0,.5,.5). We then multiply these two variables by 200 because that's the maximum value possible for those two variables.

We then need to calculate the distance between each earthquake magnitude and magnitude-time pairs. To do this, we will create a new dataset by using hclust(). We are interested in both the value and dendrogram of this object, which can be accessed with as.data.frame(object$d), where the object is the name of our hclust object.

We then use dist() to count the squared distance between each earthquake magnitude and time pair.

Dual Axis Coordinate System

Ggplot2 is a powerful and expressive plotting library for R. Its goal is to make it easy to plot data, often by reducing the code needed from the user.

This article will focus on some of the most basic ggplot2 plots, including a dual-axis coordinate system where we will plot two lines on one graph. These plots can be used for comparing two variables, for example, by plotting them on a graph.

Our data will be a series of measurements of the biological

properties of a species and the height and weight measurements of 50 mice. The columns of our data are "tissue," "age," and "weight." The rows are Mus musculus (mouse), 19 weeks and 4 grams, 2nd year of life. We can visualize these data in ggplot2 by creating a plot.

1 = Muscle 0 year old 0 grams <4
1 = Muscle 1 year old 9 grams 5-10

This plot has two lines representing two different measurement values for each mouse. However, we can also add axes to this graph to compare the two lines. We will place a line on the plot with the "shape" set to "text." This will make it possible to apply text labels to the lines that we create.

1 = Muscle 0 year old <4 grams
2 = Muscle 1 year old 9 grams 5-10 grams

This is a basic example of using ggplot2 for visualization and data comparison. We have a series of points displayed on a graph, and we can have text labels above each point that label it. You can imagine many more possibilities for plots, such as comparing data by gender or by age.

The code for this example is shown below. Save the file, load it into R and run the "plot_measurements" function.

Plot_measurements <- function(data) {

Ggplot(data, aes(x = "tissue", y = "weight")) +

Geom_point() + geom_text(aes(label = weight)) +

Ggplot(data, aes(x = "tissue", y = "age")) + geom_point() + geom_text(aes(label = age))#1

Ggplot(data, aes(x = "tissue", y = "age") –

X = "tissue", y = "weight") + geom_point() +
 theme.rug() + theme(axis.text = element_text(size = 9))#2

Ggplot(data, aes(x = "age", y = "weight") –

X = "age", y = "tissue")) + geom_point() +
 theme.rug() + theme(axis.text = element_text(size = 9))#3

Ggplot(data, aes(x = "age", y = "tissue")) +

 geom_point() + geom_line() + theme.rug() + theme(axis.text = element_text(size = 9))#4

}

The number after # is based on R's convention for numbering the function arguments. This is unnecessary, but it can help prevent any confusion. #1 tells R that there are two text labels to be added to the plot, and that label will be "age." #2 tells R which text label should be used as the axis text (muscle 0 vs. interval between muscle 0 and 1). You can also see that we have used a conditional statement here called theme(axis.text = element_text(size = 9)). This tells R to use the same text size used to make the axis labels (9).
 2. We begin by using the theme() to apply our aesthetics to our plot. The code "theme.rug" will give our lines a thickness and color gradient, much like what you would see when editing a Microsoft Word document.
 3. Here we again use the theme() to apply a different aesthetic to our plot, removing all of the points from our graph and removing any labels we may have added. You can see how this removes all of the displayed data at each point on the graph. We then add in "theme(axis.text = element_text(size = 9))" to make the axis text style consistent with the other aesthetics in the plot.

1 = Muscle 0 year old 0 grams <4
1 = Muscle 1 year old 9 grams 5-10

 2 = Muscle 2 year old 20 grams 11-20

 3 = Muscle 3 year old 37 grams >10

The following example demonstrates how to use the data frame format to display information about some species in our dataset. This is how we would specify a point on a graph, in this case, the tissue property of mice for two different species using the data frame format.

Muscle 0-year-old <4 grams
Muscle 1-year-old 9 grams 5-10 grams
Muscle 2-year-old 20 grams 11-20 grams
Muscle 3-year-old 37 grams >10 grams

We also can display information about values and trends amongst each of our variables. This can be done by including as many columns as variables that you want to have in your graph, specifying the name of each column, and then adding together all of the values in the first column.

Muscle + age = weight
Muscle + age = muscle tissue
Muscle + tissue + age = weight
Muscle tissue + age = weight

We specify the name of two variables, "muscle" and "age," and the functions that will be applied to these variables, which are the addition operator (+) and the multiplication operator (*).
 2. This is an example of what would be a trend line for our data. It has been demonstrated that there is an inverse correlation between muscle and age, so as we increase in age, muscle decreases.
 3. This combination of variables displays all the data, a trend line, and the tissue value for each mouse.

1 = Muscle 0 year old <4 grams
2 = Muscle 1 year old 9 grams 5-10 grams

3 = Muscle 2 year old 20 grams 11-20 grams
4 = Muscle 3 year old 37 grams >10 grams

This example displays information about species, age, and tissue. It would be possible to add information about sex affecting these values. We may also want to include more than two variables the same way we set up our data before, creating a data frame with multiple columns.

1 = Muscle 0 year old <4 grams
2 = Muscle 1 year old 9 grams 5-10 grams
3 = Muscle 2 year old 20 grams 11-20 grams
4 = Muscle 3 year old 37 grams >10 grams

This example displays information about species, age, and tissue. It would be possible to add information about sex affecting these values. We may also want to include more than two variables the same way we set up our data before, creating a data frame with multiple columns.

Chapter 4: Statistical Analysis in Plotting and Scatterplots with ggstatsplot (gggo)

Data visualization is a fascinating and vital part of understanding data better. It goes towards efficiently presenting the data to comprehend and share with others. It helps tell the story of data that can be hard to grasp with just numbers or words.

This article introduces the R package ggstatsplot (often referred to as gggo), an extension of the popular ggplot2 package. It makes it easy to create statistical plots, often used in data visualizations. Many plots created with this package are Line plots, Bar Plot, Histogram, Box Plot, Dot Plot, and Scatterplot.

Why ggstatsplot?

The ggstatsplot package was designed by Claude Bouvier and David Giltinan so that users can quickly produce high-quality statistical plots using R. This becomes especially helpful when dealing with large data sets of up to 100k rows or more.

To get started with gggo, one first needs to install the package like any other R package.

If you have already installed the ggplot2 package, it is possible to install ggstatsplot by using all of the same steps required for installing ggplot2. This also means that there is no need to rerun all of the functions from the top. One should run this line:

install.packages("gggo")

ggplot2 and ggstatsplot provide a variety of different aesthetics for plotting statistical plots. Statistical graphics plots are used to show relationships between variables. In ggstatsplot, this is done with the help of geom_smooth() and facet_wrap(). Geom_smooth allows you to fit smoothly through the data points, while facet_wrap lets you split the plot into several rows or columns for each group in your data. This feature comes in especially handy when compared to other plotting packages.

Like many other plotting packages, gggo can also be run directly from RStudio. There is not much difference between working with the box from within RStudio and a script. One thing that should be noted is that gggo requires the data set to be in an extended format. This means each row should represent a single observation. When comparing it to other plotting packages like ggplot2, it is essential to note that the data frame layout will look different.

The functionality of ggstatsplot takes advantage of the strengths of R, making it very easy to customize plots through the use of scales and grids. This can save a lot of time when producing graphs while also making them more appealing and uniform in appearance. One can also add multiple statistical plots to one chart using the facet_grid() function under geom_smooth(). This also makes it easy to create a more visually appealing graph.

ggstatsplot is very customizable through scales, grids, and color palettes. To make graphs easier to read, one can use scales for the range of values present in the data. Color palettes can be customized by using the color_palette() function, which allows one to select among over 20 different palettes supported by gggo. RStudio provides several predefined color palettes which can be used with ggstatsplot.

Gridlines can be added to any graph through the grid() function. This function allows one to add two types of gridlines: vertical and horizontal. These options may be changed in an attempt to make reading graphs easier. For example, grid.pos = "y" will make the y-axis have grid lines on the y-axis and not on the x-axis.

One can also control multiple settings for each graph through facet_grid(). This is done through the use of various parameters: cols and rows. For example, changing cols = "2" to cols = "2:4" allows one to change which column will be plotted and where it will be plotted in a category axis (x). Also, changing rows = 75 to rows = 25 allows one to change the placement of the categories on the category axis.

ggstatsplot can use various layouts for graphs that can come in handy when dealing with large data sets. These graphs include bar charts, dot plots, and scatterplots. The different layouts are made possible through the help of grid(), layout() and scale_continuous() functions. In this way, one can change how data will be organized on a graph. Gggo comes with several predefined layouts as well as custom options for producing custom graphs as desired via the grid(), layout(), and scale_continuous().

With gggo, one can also create 3D plots that consist of 2 or 3 graphs stacked on top of each other. This can be done through the use of the geom_3d() function. This is where one should take note that certain restrictions are put on the data that will be plotted. For instance, for a normally distributed variable, it is not possible to plot it in 3D. As another example, binned categorical variables are not supported by default when plotting them in 3D. One can still make use of this functionality when using certain options under ggstatsplot::fill_between() and ggstatsplot::fill_between_n().

ggstatsplot also makes it possible to use themes, which in turn allows one to improve the readability of statistical graphics plots through colors and labels. Themes are used to make individual plots more readable by changing colors, font size, and other aspects of the graphical display. For ggstatsplot to work, a theme object should be present in the currently active theme. This is done by loading one into memory with:

Once this is done, simply calling theme() will create a plot with the newly loaded theme object. There are three main types of themes that can be used: qualitative, quantitative, and classic themes. This allows one to change the aesthetic appearance of graphs.

One must first create an object that acts as a container for theme-specific variables and settings to create a theme.

Notably, adjusting aesthetics such as font size or colors within RStudio's default themes is not possible. This requires extra steps for customizations to be added.

Introduction to ggstatsplot

There are numerous ways to create plots with R and ggplot2- the most popular being base R graphics and lattice. As R users, it is crucial to incorporate statistical analysis in plots with ggstatsplot. This blog post includes examples of using this package in your visualization tasks.

A data analysis using ggstatsplot must start by importing the necessary packages for data manipulation, statistical calculations, plotting, and visualization. We will use a classic example of car performance that has been used before for examples on scatterplots and regression models: mtcars.

Install.packages ("mtcars")

The minimum required to package and the required ones to install it are shown below.

Library ("ggstatsplot")

We can see that other packages are also needed for this example, but we shall not need them as we will be using only one: ggplot2. In R, we can use the? Function to see all the available functions.

? What is this package? It is a package of graphics and statistical analysis tools based on ggplot2 by Hadley Wickham. ? What is this ggplot2 thing? This is a powerful software tool developed in R with over 1000 contributors. It is used to create graphics and data analysis based on a widely recognized method for statistical graphics. It is a method that allows for easy manipulation of the independent and dependent variables and their interactions. ? What does this mean? This means that with ggplot2, we can easily manipulate figures to accomplish our goals.

We begin by importing the required packages and options from the ggstatsplot below. Our dataset will be made out of previous data (car performance) using mtcars.

> Library ("ggstatsplot")

We will use a data frame called release_data, created by us before in the car performance example with car_performance. Head (release_data)

```
## mpg  hp  disp  drat  wt    qsec   vs am gear carb
1  21.0  110 3.85  2.620 16.47 0  1  4  1  4
2  21.0  177 3.70  3.780 18.61 0  1  5  0  3
3  22.8  152 3.08  3.440 17.02 0  1  5  0  3
4  21.4  105 2.76  3.460 20.22 1  1  4  1  4
5  18.7  87  3.07  3.190 19.47 0  1  4  1  5
6  18.1  146 3.76  3.420 18.00 0  1  5  0  3
```

We start by loading the ggplot2 package, a data frame and the ggstatsplot package we just installed, all with the following code:

swiss_data <- data. frame (mpg = c (21.0, 21.0, 18.7, 18.1, 18.1, 15.8), hp = c (110, 177, 152 , 105, 87 , 146, 85), disp = c (3.85, 3.70, 2.76, 3.08, 2.90 , 3. 60), drat = c (0. 22105022 4, 0. 22060039 4, 0. 22044386 4 , 0. 22046622 5, 0. 22066592 5), wt = c (2 . 620, 3 . 780, 3 . 440, 3 . 460, 2 . 620), qsec = c (0, 1, 0, 1, 1), vs = c (1, 0, 0, 1, 0), am = c (4, 7, 5, 6), gear = c (1, 4, 5, 6))

Ggplot2 is statistical software that allows us to create graphics and data analysis based on a widely recognized method for statistical graphics. It is a method that allows for easy manipulation of the independent and dependent variables and their interactions. The result of all these manipulations is a graphic-like presentation.

Ggstatsplot varies its default settings on what are visualization options. In this example, we will analyze the data by plotting them. For this example, let us first create the plot without a line of best fit. We need to set the type = "p" option using the command geom_point().

Geom_point (mapping = aes (x = mpg, y = hp), data = swiss_data, colour = "black", size = 4)

We also set 2 options on the 1-dimensional axis. This will visualize our data in a 2-dimensional plane.

To do this, we specifically select what variables we want on the x and y-axis. Setting xlab and ylab will help users directly interpret your graph from left to right, top to bottom.

Set_xlab ("mpg") set_ylab ("hp")

For the plot, we can see one straight line. This means our data is not well grouped, which will make it more challenging to create a good image. We will have to remove this line to obtain a good result. To do this, we first use the command geom_smooth().

Ggstatsplot allows us to group objects by their type and color them or not. We need to input the tools necessary for every kind of grouping and its limit to do this. In this example, we will use sepal_length for grouping by species and data in color using stat4.

Ggstatsplot defaults to group objects if they are of the same type. We can also group by other types using a wild card, like a subset. To do this, we use the jitter value. The jitter value will allow us to control the position of grouping. In this case, we select values for jitter such that we obtain good visual results.

Ggstatsplot in its default setting does not allow us to control the position of grouping within each type of grouping (sepal lengths). This is easily done here with rbinom().

Ggstatsplot also allows users to group data by color (stat4) or not (#group). For this, we need to input the color and jitter values. We also need to set the limit as an option so that it may be set according to the size of our data.

Set_colorspace ("brewer")
Set_jitter (1 : 6, 1 : 8)
Limit = 2

Ggstatsplot allows us to do other operations on data groups by the same color, such as group by stat4. We can also use more than one group at a time with a wild card, such as a subset. In this case, we operate by species and subgroup by gear. To do this, we input a value for jitter.mm with a lower limit of 1. This means that we will be able to group our data by species and subgroup by gear within each type of grouping.

Ggstatsplot allows users to analyze data on which groups are in the same type of grouping through dendrogram. In this case, we used by color where all the values on the x-axis are colored black together, thus allowing us to see what groups are in the same type of grouping with ease.

Ggstatsplot then allows us to group by stat4 and color. To do this, we use jitter.

Ggstatsplot allows users to analyze data on which groups are in the same type of grouping through dendrogram. In this case, we used by color where all the values on the x-axis are colored black together, thus allowing us to see what groups are in the same type of grouping with ease.

Ggstatsplot then allows us to group by stat4 and color. To do this, we use jitter.

Ggstatsplot allows users to perform other operations specific to each type of grouping or not. For example, we can add labels and change font size using the option title. In this case, we use jitter to position the labels.

Ggstatsplot allows users to add a line of best fit using geom_smooth(). In this case, we limit our data to groups in the same type of grouping and use jitter so that they are more organized. We also group by data and color, as seen on the dendrogram.

Then we plot the graphic and save it.

We can then use other options of ggplot2 for our specific purposes with the following code: par (from = c (2, 2)) 1+ may be replaced with 1 – where positive means top left, negative means bottom right.

Ggplot (swiss_data, aes (x = mpg, y = hp)) + geom_point () + geom_smooth (method = lm) + scale_x_continuous (trans = "reverse") + scale_y_continuous (trans = "reverse")

We can then add our line of best fit on top of the plot by using the command coord_cartesian(xlim=c(1,20), ylim=c(23,22)) prior to adding geom_smooth().

Ggplot2 allows us to do much more with its wide range of options. However, we have presented some of the options that we can use with ggstatsplot, thus allowing us to understand the ggstatsplot framework.

Writing your functions:

In this example, we will create a simple function that does a valid linear regression for our data. The command for linear regression in R is lm(). This stands for the linear model. We could use this command when we want to formalize our relationship. In this case, we will create a simple function called reg. This will allow us to perform a linear regression on any data using our function reg. First, we need to input the data set. We will use the base R function read. This will automatically follow dependencies using this function.

Library (NutshellR) #Read data library (ggplot2) x_data <- read.csv ("~/Desktop/swiss_data.csv", colClasses = c ("factor", "integer")) y_data <- read.csv ("~/Desktop/swiss_data.csv", colClasses = c ("factor", "integer"))

Once we have our data ready, we can create our function using the following command, which stands for write(object). This function is named our function reg. This function takes x and y as arguments, where x is the data set (data), and y is the dependent variable (y). The command par(mfrow=c(1,1)) allows us to create multiple plots.

Reg <- function (x,y){ # Input values of independent variables x2 <- x$mpg # Input values of dependent variables y2 <- y$hp # Create independent variables x_inputs = c (1 : 2,rep (2, length.out= nrow (x))) # Create dependent variables y_inputs = c (1 : 2,rep (3, length.out= nrow (y))) # Set up our independent variables x_inputs <- setNames (x_inputs, names (x)) # Set up dependent variables y_inputs <- setNames (y_inputs, names (y)) # Create linear model regmodel <- lm(y2 ~ x2) # Output results return (regmodel) }

In this case, we use the function to calculate a linear regression on mpg and hp. We can then use our function reg to perform a linear regression on any data set. Note that we are returning our function as remodeled. We will discuss the return value of our function in the next section.

The output of this command would be regmodel. This stands for the regression model. In this case, y2 is the dependent variable, and x2 is the independent variable. We need to calculate regmodel by using lm(). This stands for the linear model. We then return regmodel. We need to use the command return() to produce a result.

Reg(x_datampg, y_datahp) #finds linear regression on mpg and hp

The output of this command would look like the following: object 'reg' not found. If you get this error, you probably forgot to input the function name in the hole where you are performing a calculation. For example, if I forget to input my function name as reg, I will get an error.

This section discussed a few functions in R. We then created a function by using the command reg to perform a linear regression. We also learned how to create functions using the command that follows, which stands for write(object). This function is named our function reg.

Statistical Analyses with ggstatsplot

The ggstatsplot package provides extensions of the base plotting functions from the popular ggplot2 package to enable statistical data analysis. The idea is to provide a convenient graphical interface for exploratory analysis or an intuitive first step in a data visualization pipeline.

Ggstatsplot provides several plots for visualizing statistical analyses, many of them showing graphical summaries of vital inferential statistics, such as the population mean and variance estimators, confidence intervals for the population mean, and one-sample t-test with associated p-values or histogram plots from which you can extract density estimates at specific points.

Ggstatsplot is available from CRAN and can be loaded quickly into the R environment by loading the ggstatsplot package. All functions provided by ggstatsplot are essentially wrappers around native R functions, and as such, we can use them in conjunction with any existing R packages as well as custom-written code.

It is important to remember that these plots should not be used in place of a more thorough investigation of a given dataset or set of analyses but are intended to provide a graphical summary of results that may be useful when communicating with other researchers, reviewers, or presentation audiences.

All of the plots are available via the plot function. All plots are controlled through a single object that provides access to the title, axes, controls, and plot settings. Plots can be created in any order, and each plot appears on a new page when viewed with RStudio.

Plotting Statistics in R

The ggstatsplot package provides two types of statistical graphs: a scatter plot and a histogram. You can customize the x-axis range, y-axis range, titles, labels, cross-references, and vertical scaling for each type of graph. Ggstatsplot provides a number of plot templates for various statistics and inferential tests, as well as ways to customize the plots completely.

To create the plot, use the function name, such as "ggstatsplot:::scatter" or "ggstatsplot:::histogram." The plot functions will produce a statistical plot that can be customized in many ways, including elements for descriptive statistics, the test results examined, and a brief test description.

After adjusting one or more settings using the arguments or using several helper functions to help with specific elements, you can then set up plots using RStudio. If you work in RStudio, you can define most plot settings within a single RStudio environment. Use the "ggstatsplot:::set" function and then use "ggstatsplot:::plot" to draw your plot.

Multiple plots can be created at once using the "ggstatsplot:::addplot", "ggstatsplot:::addhist" or "ggstatsplot:::addscatter" functions. You can also combine these functions to modify multiple plots in one step. Other features include setting a default palette and controls. The default palette is accessed through the "ggstatsplot:::palette" function. Scatter plots allow you to build small-scale plots quickly and easily, with multiple options for axis labels, line thicknesses, and other aspects of the plot design. Histograms are particularly useful for analyzing the distribution of data and evaluating skewness. The ggstatsplot package also provides the basic range, density, and kernel density estimation plots needed to complete a visualization pipeline.

What's new in ggstatsplot? The current version of ggstatsplot (0.1) is still considered experimental and should be used with some caution. Having said that, many common types of plots and statistics can be executed using the provided functions. Future versions will expand the capabilities as more users adopt this approach.

Functions available in ggplot2 can be used with the ggstatsplot package but typically require some modification. Functions from other packages can also be used as long as they can be called and are applied to a two-dimensional dataset. The plot settings for all functions are controlled through a single object that has access to multiple levels of control via axes, the main title, axis titles, and axis controls.

A new function called "ggstatsplot:::setup" is used for setting up plots in RStudio.

The scatter plot template can be customized to create simple distributions and histograms. The scatter plot functions are controlled through a single object that has access to multiple levels of control via axes, labels, and the main title.

The customizations available with the scatter plot include the following items: y-axis limit, x-axis range, title, labels, error bars, and annotation. There are also options for adjusting the color and size of points.

The histogram template allows you to specify a date range, main axis title, and primary axis annotations. The histogram functions are controlled through a single object that has access to multiple levels of control via axes, the main title, labels, and annotation.

Kernel density estimation plots can be created with a template or through customization. The kernel density estimates are controlled through a single object that has access to multiple levels of control via axes and the main title.

There are four basic types of kernel density plots available: "ggstatsplot:::kde", "ggstatsplot:::density", "ggstatsplot:::density2" and "ggstatsplot:::rug". Each function accepts a normalization parameter, allowing for different color schemes for different datasets.

The following functions are available for a given plot to create variations of the default plot. These functions will take an additional argument of either "palette" or "viewport" to control colors and sizes. By default, the functions take both 'palette' and 'viewport' arguments. If you do not want to use either of these color schemes, set them to NULL. This package is intended for use with R-Studio and requires an R-Studio connection already present when using this package in an R environment.

Chapter 5: Visualization and Model Interpretation

Most data visualizations in R begin with the qplot function. It is important to note that not just any old plot can be created with qplot. To create a three-dimensional plot, you first need to identify the y coordinate axis and then specify something called a stacking method. There are two options for stacking methods: "front" and "back." A front rendering displays the first set of points in the order they appear in your data, whereas a back rendering displays the last set of points.

One important use of the qplot function is to manipulate your data to make it visually appealing. In particular, you can use the fit and fill tools to obtain a better visual representation of your points. The easiest way of setting the default viewport is by passing a list of x-axis ranges to the set viewport command.

The main advantage of using qplot over ggplot2 is that you do not need to specify any other graphical device drivers. It is also good to use qplot for small data sets because it is easier to work with than ggplot2.

The "qplot Assistants" package allows you to create data visualizations through an interactive GUI rather than writing code. The software requires R version 3.1 or later and is run from the R console.

The qplot Assistant software enables you to select your data, visualize it in a cross-platform interface, and save it in various formats for later use. You can request multiple visualizations through the qplot Assistant software, and each visualization can be saved in any format or customized in any way you want. You can change the title and axis labels, choose the type of chart to create, and add a box plot, density plots, and histograms to your visualization. The Assistant comes with many pre-set formats in which you can save your data.

The qplot Assistant package also allows you to integrate into the R software through two specific packages called qtiles and rCharts. You can also send custom command parameters directly to other visualization packages within R without writing any code.

To use the qplot Assistant software, you have to run it from the R console and go through all of the options it offers for creating data visualizations. The Assistant can be used by any user with R version 3.1 or later.

This package is a front-end for other R packages such as gridExtra, gtable, and ggplot2. It was developed so that new users could easily build applications that use the full power of R without having to learn how to code any functions or accomplish them through detailed specifications. The package uses the same underlying code that qplot uses, but it is essentially a different interface for writing visualizations. It allows you to insert graphics into documents and send them to nine different output formats, including PDF, PNG, and TIFF. You can use it to create reports.

You can install the qtiles package by typing the following into the R console:

Install.packages("qTables")

The best point size to use when you generate a visualization in R depends on the type of graphic. For bar charts and histograms, 5- or 6-point font size is preferred because it gives a clear view of the data points while allowing enough space between them. If you want to include legends on your charts, use 8- or 9-point font size because too much space between characters makes it hard to read. For scatterplots and box plots, a 12-point font size is acceptable for good visual clarity. For plots with many text labels, use font size 16 or 18.

The R software is a helpful tool for data visualization, yet it is not always easy to learn and use. As a result, users who do not have time to learn R may find it challenging to create the best-performing visualizations. At the same time, companies looking for an effective way to display their data may also find it challenging to identify the right tool for the job. This is where qplot Assistants comes into play. The package allows users to create data visualizations quickly through its cross-platform and interactive interface without writing code or installing any other applications or packages on their computers. As a result, data visualization can be completed in minutes rather than weeks or months. The package helps users produce data visualizations of various types using one single destination. It can also display data on multiple platforms, including Windows, Mac, and Linux systems.

The qplot assistants' package allows users to create their interactive and cross-platform graphical elements such as treemaps and bubble charts quickly through various design templates based on statistical and non-statistical data visualization models. These designs are readily available from the templates section with an extensive collection of templates for different sales, inventory management, medicine, and computer science applications.

Graphical Model Visualization

R Data visualization is a package of functions to create and explore 3d scatterplots, heatmaps, and other graphs in R.

The package contains data visualization functions and methods for creating plots in R related to statistical models. The graphical model visualizations include the following: boxplot, bar chart, probability density plot (PDP), and binary logistic regression fit graph. There is also some other non-graphical model-related functionality, such as plotting scatterplots with many variables.

Visualization is used to explore relationships between variables in complex graphical models. It helps visualize the interaction of different variables and understand how they affect each other. Visualization is also helpful for identifying atypical observations in a dataset and for letting you examine global trends in the data.

On the other hand, model interpretation involves fitting statistical models and comparing their output to actual data to help answer questions about data. R Data Visualization can be especially useful in this context as it can be used to generate graphs that help us understand how a model fits our data.

R Data Visualization was initially conceived to fit probability density plots (PDPs) in R to data. Later, the package was expanded to include a broader scope of functionality. While using R Data Visualization for fitting PDPs, it is also possible to create other types of graphs with the functions and methods provided by this package.

R Data visualization helps create 3D scatter plots and 2D histograms, bar charts, box plots, bar charts, PDPs, etc. It follows the same syntax as ggplot2 but includes many new options not found in ggplot2.

The package was contributed by Johannes Trefzer and is part of the more significant RModeler project. This package aims to make using 3d scatterplots and 2d histograms in R quicker and easier. It also provides a framework for creating new data visualization functions related to statistical models. R Data visualization has the following features:

Data visualization is used in various projects and fields, including statistical modeling, machine learning, drug design, etc.

It is possible to visualize multiple variables and show how they affect each other. This is useful for showing relationships in a dataset and understanding how different variables affect the results. It can also identify unusual observations in a dataset and examine global trends.

R Data visualization helps generate plots in R that help investigate statistical models, explore different hypotheses, and predict new data sets.

Model Interpretation means fitting mathematical/statistical models to data to answer questions about the data. R Data Visualization can be especially useful for generating graphs that help us understand how a model fits our data.

Graphical models have become very popular, and there are different packages in R for fitting them. R Data visualization makes it possible to visualize the results of model fitting. Because of this, it could be helpful for practitioners interested in data visualization and model interpretation.

Other packages let you create 3D scatterplots in R like mclust, factoextra, rgl, and 3dvis. However, they do not provide the functionality offered by R Data Visualization.

The following example shows how to install and use R Data visualization to create a scatterplot with many variables:

Code:

```
# InstallRDataVisualization package from CRAN using install.packages() function
Install.packages("RDataVisualization")
# Load the Package into R using library() function
Library(RDataVisualization)
# Create a scatterplot with many variables
Plot.many(mtcars, x = mpg, y = disp, z = wt)
```

The following example shows how to create a 2D histogram in R using R Data visualization and ggplot2:

Code:

…
```
# Define model
Model = rlogit(formula = gender ~ ., data = dataset)
# Fit this model and get the results
Fit = model.fit(dataset)
# Plot the results using ggplot2
Ggplot(dataset, aes(x = prob, y = count)) + geom_histogram(bins = 30) + labs(title = "Created using R Data visualization and ggplot2"
```

Data visualization is an essential part of any analysis. Before any data can be analyzed, it must first be encoded into a visual display such as a table or graph. The quality of graphical displays can dramatically affect the usefulness of data for understanding and reasoning about natural phenomena. For example, when we want to understand the distribution of medical expenditures per person per year in Canada broken down by province and age group, we will likely find a histogram much more helpful than a table of numbers:

Graphical displays represent data based on properties independent of quantitative values (e.g., color, shape, size). This allows for an easier comparison of visual patterns and trends among different data sets. They are also more intuitive and visually appealing than a table of numerical values. Effective visualization is an essential part of understanding data.

The main components of a graphical model are:

Graphical data models have been developed using abstract concepts such as networks, hypergraphs, nested graphs, directed acyclic graphs (DAGs or digraphs), multigraphs, or representations in computer science such as graphs of functions, produced treemaps or charts of objects/properties.

Graphical models are extracted from data and represented as an image. In their simplest form, they are either a scatter plot or a bar graph, in which each dimension of the original data is mapped to one or multiple visual dimensions such as position, size, and color. More complex graphs are constructed by combining several simple graphs inconsistent ways.

In addition to simple visualization methods such as scatterplots and histograms, more sophisticated statistical graphics such as parallel coordinates plots have been developed. Another example of a graphical display is glyphs with minimum overlap (properties like violin plots) to show the distribution of data points when we want to compare multiple categories at once. Other examples include circle pack plots and treemaps.

A Scatter plot is a simple graphing method to show how two variables are related. In a scatter plot, the horizontal axis represents the values of one variable, and the vertical axis shows the corresponding values for the second variable.

A histogram shows how often different values of a variable (e.g., age) are present in a set (e.g., population). It is an intuitive way to display data distribution that can be used to alternate plots like box plots that don't consider all categories equally.

Graphical models are standard in many application areas such as data analysis, data warehouses, and social networking. They can be used for data visualization as well. Visualization methods used in these areas can be broken down into two categories: static and dynamic. Static methods focus on the visual aspects of visualization, such as its display. In contrast, active strategies focus on how to get the data from a source (data warehouse) and then transform it to provide meaningful visualizations.

Statistical modeling is a process that starts with an idea and ends with an empirical test that can be used to either confirm or reject a hypothesis. Different approaches can be applied depending on the problem area, the nature of the data, and the desired level of accuracy. One approach to statistical modeling is data mining, a form of big data where clusters of related variables are formed using algorithms. The cluster definitions can be visualized using machine learning methods such as clustering algorithms. This approach can be used to discover hidden patterns in a dataset.

VisTrails is an open-source tool that allows the user to create interactive, web-based visualizations which can be shared and saved. The resulting images are called dynamic displays. They will enable the user to zoom in or out of different subregions and interact with them by changing the transparency of specific data points or performing histogram-based queries.

To make these displays interactive, various methods need to be applied, such as:

VisTrails uses d3.js, which allows for more flexibility when creating graphic models. It also provides transitions, animations, mouse interactions, and more.

Interpretation of the Data and Predictions

Another excellent visualization is to extract a heatmap of the data based on the most frequent value. The intensity of color corresponds with how many instances of that value occurred in the sample. We can now see which values are most frequent in the sample by looking at their respective intensities for this data set. Readers might notice that these two charts provide different pictures for some values. The bar chart would show no uncommon values, whereas the heat map shows very few occurrences and one instance in Dark Brown (fourth row, second position) for each column/row, respectively.

This is a variation of the heatmap. Instead of showing how many values appeared, we will indicate which values occurred most frequently. Therefore, this plot emphasizes the common values and helps the viewer understand the meaning behind their frequencies.

This visualization employs a different type of cartogram. The content is the same, but only the size (area) is changed.

Several charts are available for the textual data made in the previous section. The data is visualized as a bar chart or disc rectangle. However, it has been seen that the data visualization could be enhanced by introducing color and unique labels. This visualization shows how well each region of interest fits into the population.

The Data-to-Chart Communication Model

There are two types of communication depending on whether the two parties are face-to-face or not: verbal and visual. In this example, the chart communicates information to the reader. This can be done simply by labeling each line ascending or descending order. It is also possible to speak of this type of communication as representing how effective the title is to support the reader in understanding the data displayed below. When designing data visualized charts, you want to ensure that each chart is viewed by someone who has never seen it before and does not understand what it represents.

The Visual Message

When constructing data visualization, we want to make sure each chart makes a clear visual statement about its underlying subject. When designing data visualization, you want to make sure that each chart is being viewed by someone who has never seen it before and does not have an understanding of what it represents. However, that's not to say that the reader can't be familiar with your analysis's subject or general message. In this research paper, one must be familiar with the geography and population distribution of England/the United Kingdom to understand its contents.

Below are charts and what they represent:

Choropleth Map – This map uses colors to show relative population density. In this case, Dark Blue (third row, first position) appears for almost the entire country, and Dark Orange (third row, third position) for a country with a very high population density.

Cartogram – A cartogram uses the combination of a circle and a square to represent a relative area (cartographic projection). This displays the distribution of countries by size relative to each other based on their population sizes.

DotPlot – The dot plot is a famous.jo chart for showing frequencies. A dot plotted graph visualizes the data in categories and represents them by the number of occurrences.

Histogram – The histogram is a variation of the dot plot but with a different distribution. The histogram uses joint distributions instead of a simple vertical line.

Box plots or box and whisker plots are vector graphics that use rectangles and whiskers to highlight specific data points like outliers or extreme values. In this case, we can see the middle 50%, which is called the interquartile range, represented by light blue (third row, third position).

Pie Chart – Pie charts show a breakdown of the whole and their shares relative to each other. The pie chart breaks down the populations by country and shows their respective percentages.

TreeMap – A treemap is a different type of cartogram that uses a tree instead of a square or circle to show relative area. This is an alternative to the choropleth map because it allows readers to get insights into regions instead of countries or states. In this case, Dark Green (third row, second position) represents the highest population density, followed by Dark Orange (third row, third position). We can also see that India is relatively denser than China.

Cluster Map – Cluster maps help show countries' relative population by size. Dark Blue (third row, first position) has a much larger close area than Dark Orange (third row, third position).

Radar Chart – Radar charts use a circular pie chart-like diagram. Each slice in the pie chart represents a portion of a whole represented by data in the parts. In this case, if each country is considered a portion of the entire world population, Dark Blue (third row, first position) would represent about 0.25% of the world population, and Dark Orange (third row, third position) would represent approximately 0.23% of the world population. The step from 0.23% to 0.

Composite Chart – Composite charts use a combination of bars, dot plots, and pie charts. The readings are presented in bars, while the percentages are shown through dot plots or pie charts.

Gantt Chart – A Gantt chart uses vertical lines to show the sequence of activities involved in the project. Each cell represents one activity, and the length of a cell shows time. Dark Blue (third row, first position) has a long time, and Dark Orange (third row, third position) has a short time on its side.

Disaggregated Chart – A Disaggregated Chart is a bar chart where the bars show percentages or ranks of values. In this example, we see the highest 10% (Dark Blue, first row) and the lowest 10% (Dark Green, second row) represent a total population of 66 million people, while the middle 50% is mentioned in Dark Red (third row).

Pie Chart Skeleton – A pie chart skeleton is similar to the pie chart with one difference: instead of showing percentages or ranks, it uses dots to indicate how much each share or rank represents in a particular category.

Pie Chart Pyramid – A Pie Chart Pyramid presents data as a pyramid compared to a regular pie chart. This way of visualizing data allows the reader to get a clearer idea of the interrelations with each other.

Stacked Bar Chart – A stacked bar chart combines a stacked graph and a bar chart. The stacked graph represents the same data in an alternative format. This is also called a multiple bar graph because each bar can be considered many individual datasets over time.

Interaction – An interaction visualization gives readers the ability to manipulate parts of an image that contains information to explore or discover hidden patterns or relationships that show how variations affect outcomes or vice versa.

Ribbon Chart – A ribbon chart is a representation of hierarchal information. The series of bars and the colors used to show them are just a simple way to show interaction in hierarchical form without using multiple graphs.

Chapter 6: External Libraries

The two libraries most commonly used with data visualization are ggplot2 and d3.js.

Ggplot2 is a plotting system for summarizing data, ideal for showing trends and patterns in the data.

D3.js is an open-source JavaScript library for manipulating documents based on data. Unlike the base graphics system in R, which is limited to static graphics, D3 can update and change according to user interaction or streaming data sources such as web socket connections (and unlike with HTML/JavaScript, there are no cross-domain restrictions).

Because of the complexity of visualizing data, there are many packages available in R.

The graphics package was developed as part of an attempt by statisticians to provide a standard graphics system for statistical applications. Originally, graphics for statistical applications were written in Fortran or Basic, which made it difficult for different programs to communicate with each other. Additionally, these applications were not "portable" across platforms or languages. The goal of the graphics package was to provide a better interface between users and the computer. It also aimed to improve efficiency to complete more computations while generating a plot.

The graphics package is a relatively simple one that uses ASCII characters to generate plots. The operating system performs the actual plotting of the characters. Three "types" of graphics are defined: functions, axes, and points. Functions generate a curve, and axes generate one or more coordinate axes (generally shown on the "x"- and "y"-axes). Points can be created with or without coordinates.

R provides many functions for generating data graphs in base graphics; several graphic devices can be used to plot graphs, including X11 and svg. Using what R calls "the grammar of graphics," users can create vectors composed of values at points on an axis. Arithmetic operators can then be applied to these vectors. These operations, which include arithmetic and logical operations, allow for the creation of complex graphs.

Many packages extend the graphics package. One of the most popular is ggplot2, a reformulation of base graphics in terms of "grammars" and "devices." It allows for different types of axes, including multiple types for an individual axis, and supports more complex graphs than base graphics.

Ggplot2 can be used with multiple data sets simultaneously, for example, in a web browser window or when using an R session on a remote computer to display two or more data sets from two different hosts. This capability is similar to how the HTML5 canvas works on Windows and Mac OS X platforms.

Other packages can be used to create charts and graphs, including lattice and Cairo.

D3.js is used to create web graphics and visualizations; this library is well suited to R because of its ability to read data from the console and a "clipboard." Data visualization with D3 requires the use of different components: selections (which select data), scales (which determine how values are mapped onto the plot), axes (which mark the coordinate systems on which data points are plotted), and finally, a series of append operations that add elements such as lines, shapes or text to the graph.

The R programming language supports multi-threaded programming through its parallel package. This package has several different capabilities, including defining similar functions or functions that will run in parallel without specifying an explicit number of threads that will run the function. A combiner function is also available to combine results from multiple iterations in a parallel loop. This ability to handle multiple threads has become increasingly important as computers have increased in processing power and been able to host more than one CPU. The ability to run different functions in parallel enables R users to take advantage of this increased processing power.

One common form of parallelization is the case where a task can be split into chunks, each of which can be run on a separate processor. In these situations, there are two ways that R uses multiple processors. The first is when R uses a single thread to perform all the work across multiple CPUs – this approach does not have much impact on increasing performance as it still has one thread for all CPUs. The other approach is to use one thread for every CPU – this way effectively allows 100% utilization of each processor.

There are four primary tools in R for parallelization. These include the snow, MPI, and threads packages and the foreach package in recent versions of R.

The snow package is a collection of tools that can be used to distribute work in R over a cluster of computers. It includes parallel versions of many functions from the base language and offers particular constructs specialized for distributed work under the control of a master process. All computations are performed within child processes, and communication occurs via message passing between these processes. The MPI package consists of functions that allow for the communication of messages between processes. Pthreads is an R package that uses POSIX threads to communicate between parallel processes. The final package is for each, a unique construct used to control the flow of data across multiple processors.

How data sets can be accessed varies greatly depending on what type of database or database management system (DBMS) a programmer chooses. Some database management systems are more suitable for analytic needs, including those where it is desirable to impose restrictions on the data sets analyzed; others are less suited for analytics but provide more comprehensive data storage, query, and reporting capabilities than many other types of database systems. DBMSs provide more data storage and more capabilities for reporting results. A typical DBMS in use today is provided by the MySQL family of products. There are many variants of MySQL, including free open-source software; commercial versions of MySQL, such as the Oracle version; and several proprietary options, some of which are available at no cost to the end-user while others charge a fee for certain services, such as creating and managing databases.

Some aspects specific to R can be accessed through unique interfaces with DBMSs. For example, R provides functions that allow R to perform queries against the database system so that information can be retrieved or stored as a result.

Creating Visualizations with Other Packages

Visualizations are an integral part of data analysis. They allow us to explore the properties of the data, compare different datasets and identify patterns that may not be apparent with just tables and summaries. Visualizations are a powerful means to explore our data. Still, to do so effectively, we need appropriate tools – many packages exist for this purpose, each with its advantages and limitations.

In this post, we'll introduce some of the most commonly used visualization methods (using ggplot2), go through what's needed for their implementation in R, and highlight some other options you can use as well when you find yourself lacking the desired package or to make use of your preferred color scheme.

Why Use ggplot2?

Why use ggplot2 out of all the other data visualization options in R? It's an excellent question and a favorite topic of discussion on r/R, r/dataisbeautiful, and other communities in the social media sphere. There are many great answers to this, but here's one: With ggplot2, you can create customized visualizations using a minimal number of steps. You won't need to code them! This is largely missing from most other data visualization packages in R.

Let's look at an example of how to use ggplot2 to create a basic graph. I've created a package that contains the minimum code you need to get started for your convenience. You can install it from GitHub using this line:

Install.packages("ggplot")

Now, let's go to the R console and see what the first few lines do:

Library(ggplot2) library(tidyverse) library(…your specific dataset…) ## # A tibble: 1 × 2 ## # Groups: dataset [1] grouping variable value ## <chr> <dbl> <chr> ## 1 First Value 1.5 ## # … with 1 more variables: `value` <dbl>

Pretty straightforward, right? Let's look at what this code does in detail. The first line imports the ggplot2 package and its "core" functions. The second line is a comment that tells R to ignore the rest of the code being written and skips it directly to $data = as.Tibble() . Here we're just telling R that our dataset is an object of class tibble, a tidy data structure that can be used with other tidy packages (like tibbleExtra) and will be visible throughout. The last two lines use the dataset's grouping variables to specify the visualization. Here we can see that each dataset column is coded by `variable.` Our grouping variable is `grouping,` and our value is `value.`

So, why is ggplot2 so customizable? Where does this code get executed? To understand that, we need to understand where R code gets executed. R has three different environments where code must be executed: global, package, and session. Global functions are executed when you first log in to R. This is the code that starts when you first open an R session by typing:

R

➢   R >

A package is where you will execute the code that you've written in a package. A package is a set of files that are saved in your working directory (by default:

~/Documents/my_projects/ ….) and its relative path to the R executable (/Users/david/.R/the_packages_folder). So, let's open our project's working directory from within R. We can do this using ls (including the `-l` flag for listing more than one file) or by typing dir.

➢   Ls #> [1] "dataset.RData" "tidyverse/tidyverse.R" > R > dir() #> [1] "~/Documents/bags/dataset" "~/Documents/bags/dataset.RData" "~/Documents/bags/tidyverse/"

Now that we're in our project's working directory, let's create our package by typing:

R > . . / bags / dataset / dataset.RData

Now, I can use the newly created dataset object in my R session to create visualizations. Let's try it out on our previous example with ggplot2:

R > library (ggplot2) R > library (tidyverse) R > library (datasets) R > # loading `tidyverse` previously added `ggplot2` to the global environment R > # loading `datasets` previously added `tibble` to the global environment R > . . / bags / dataset / dataset #> Loading required package : tidyverse #> Loading required package : ggplot2 #> Loaded tidyverse : 1.1 . 1 #> Loading required package : datasets #> Loaded datasets : 1.2 . 0

With the code library.dynam(), we can see that the ggplot2 package has been added to our global environment __GlobalEnv__ via load_all() . The tidyverse and datasets packages were also added to our global environment. The previous snippet of code doesn't tell us where it was executed. To find that out, we can type what() . It tells us that the code was executed in the global environment, not in a package and that it's now visible to any other function I write.

R > what () #> [1] "/Users/david/.R/the_packages_folder/ggplot2/library.dynam" #> [2] "/Users/david/.R/the_packages_folder/tidyverse-1.1.1" #> [3] "/Users/david/.R/the_packages_folder/datasets-1.2.0" #> [4] "/Users/david/.R/the_global_environment__GlobalEnv__"

If we want to use our function within the package where it is defined, then there's more that needs to be done. First, let's get into the working directory:

R > ## switching to working directory R > dir () #> [1] "~/Documents/bags/dataset" "~/Documents/bags/" #> [3] "~/.RData" "~/.Renv" #> [5] "~/.Renviron" "~/.mongorc.site" #> [8] "~/Documents/bags/"

Ok, now let's create our dataset object:

R > library (tidyverse) R > library (ggplot2) R > db <- dataset (list (a1 = 1, a2 = 2, b1 = 3, b2 = 4), stringsAsFactors = F) #> Call: ## S4 method for classes 'tibble' and 'matrix': tidy_tables(x, names=...) ## ... db #> <data.frame [3 x 3]> #> NA #> <chr> <dbl> <chr> #> 1 1.5 2 2 3 4

Now we can use our function using db :

R > what (db) #=> 2.0.0

But ggplot2 won't use our function. We can see that by typing:

R > db #> <data.frame [3 x 3]> #> NA #> <chr> <dbl> <chr> #> 1 1.5 2 2 3 4 R > ggplot (aes (a1, b1)) + geom_point () #=> Warning message: There was a problem when calling the conversion function "tidy_tables". The returned value didn't have class "tidy" and was assigned to the wrong class namespace. # This warning is shown once per session; to suppress it, use cleanup .

So, what's wrong with ggplot2? If you remember, we had to tell R that our dataset is an object of class tibble . So, let's try that out:

R > db <- -> tidy_tables (list (a1 = 1, a2 = 2, b1 = 3, b2 = 4), stringsAsFactors = F) #> Call: #> .local(x) #> #> db <data.frame [3 x 3]> <chr> <dbl> <chr> #> 1 1.5 2 2 3 4

Now, let's try and use our function with ggplot2 :

R > ggplot (aes (x = a1, y = b1)) + geom_point () #=> Warning message: There was a problem when calling the conversion function "tidy_tables". The returned value didn't have class "tidy" and was assigned to the wrong class namespace. # This warning is shown once per session; to suppress it, use cleanup . R > db <- -> tidy_tables (list (a1 = 1, a2 = 2, b1 = 3, b2 = 4), stringsAsFactors = F) #<data.frame [3 x 3]> #> NA #> <chr> <dbl> <chr> #> 1 1.5 2 2 3 4 R > ggplot (aes (x = a1, y = b1)) + geom_point () #=> Warning message: Missing values are always removed by `geom_point()` .

The result is similar to before, but now ggplot2 Is getting the correct code. However, if you try to plot something, you'll notice that we still get the same warning message because we're still missing values in our dataset. We can fix that using the fill argument:

R > ggplot (aes (x = a1, y = b1, fill = a2)) + geom_point () #=> Warning message: Missing values are always removed by `geom_point()` . R > db <- -> tidy_tables (list (a1 = 1, a2 = 2, b1 = 3, b2 = 4), stringsAsFactors = F) #> Call: #> .local(x) #> #> db <data.frame [3 x 3]> <chr> <dbl> <chr> #> 1 1.5 2 2 3 4 R > ggplot (aes (x = a1, y = b1, fill = a2)) + geom_point () #=> Warning message: Missing values are always removed by `geom_point()` .

We want to remove the warning message because the function ggplot2 uses the function tidy_tables, and if we're missing lines that use it, it will cause errors. To remove that warning message, we can add a line. Renviron :

R > . . / bags / dataset / dataset #> Loading required package : tidyverse #> Loading required package : ggplot2 #> Loaded tidyverse : 1.1 .

R Markdown Template

As with many other packages in R, there are some pre-made examples and a template. RStudio provides the R markdown package, the default editor when working with gggo, or any package created using R Markdown. It can be used to generate an Rmd file for publication, as well as for open-access publication.

The layout of the template files is pretty basic and has very little documentation, so there might be a lot of questions related to how to use these files for publication purposes properly.

Here is an example of the template file for making a vignette:

\documentclass{article} \usepackage{amsmath,amssymb} \begin{document} \begin{frame} % If you would rather not have the header in this article, delete this line and use \vspace*{0.25in}\hspace*{6pt}\vspace*{0.25in}\hspace*{6pt}\vspace*{0.25in}\hspace*{6pt}\par %\endframe % If you would rather not have the footer in this article remove this line and use \endfooter… etc. etc… %....some text… % In the beginning of the file you can use \usepackage{somepackage} to include some package, if you would like to include another one that is not included By default in this template: \usepackage{lipsum} %....some text...\end{document}

The vignette or mini papers have become more popular because they have a lot of extra valuable information for beginners trying to learn any particular field. A paper typically includes all the sources and methods used to complete research; however, vignettes generally are longer than a regular journal article and incorporate much of what is needed to analyze correctly.

One issue that currently plagues vignettes is the lack of access. Many universities will not pay for journal subscriptions to view these articles, and some people find it easier to read through them in their entirety on Google Drive. Due to this issue, a new format can be used in conjunction with R Markdown called "book down." The main benefit of using a book down over vignette is the ease of accessibility. This format is also known as open-source publishing because all files are available at once, rather than accessing them one by one. However, they take much longer than a traditional paper to write out and construct properly. The layout is also different than a conventional paper, as there are more graphical elements and more emphasis on consistency.

The overall process used to make a book down starts the same as for a vignette. The data, code, and text sections are all incorporated into an Rmd file, which can be viewed in RStudio or other software that utilizes the R Markdown format. However, one of the most critical things that need to be done is creating a LaTeX document which will be converted into PDF format. This document needs to have the same layout of each element as those in the RMD file. At the beginning of the document, it is also essential to include information about how many columns, subheadings, figures, tables, etc. The RMD files are the source documents, which means that they are typically not published themselves.

The entire book is then converted into an e-book using LaTeX2e and a " bibe program," which converts all data into a bibtex file. Once this has been done and published on a website, it can be accessed in several ways. It can be viewed directly through HTML or downloaded in PDF format.

Universities and research groups use R Markdown to create book-length manuscripts for publication. One of the challenges in this area is that many students or professors will typically only publish a manuscript once their Ph.D. is complete. Due to this, not all of the best parts of each paper will be preserved, making it hard to navigate through.

Another problem is that results are often used multiple times during a project, and if they are published right away, other people might decide to use the same data. Many times this will result in a paper duplication issue. As a result, some papers won't be published until after completing a peer-review process. Related to this, many of these books are not published in a way that encourages the reader to use the data and code quickly, so there is a good chance that it may be incorrectly used.

Data science is a vast field, as it includes programming and statistics. Until recently, the data science community could share these results through traditional journal articles and online blogs (such as the "R-Bloggers" site). However, there has been a movement from those who feel that R Markdown can be used to create walkthroughs of various analyses that are more useful than an article or a blog post for sharing techniques. Many of these new formats have been designed to be easily accessible for learning purposes. These newer formats include blogs and articles, which are much easier to read and share than traditional documents due to their interactive nature.

There are two main ways of publishing the data and code used in R

Markdown-based manuscripts. The first way is to include the data and regulations within the manuscript. In this case, you would have all of the necessary files in a separate directory (if different than the manuscript directory) and reference it directly.

The second option is to have an external website providing access to the materials used in the analysis and a detailed walkthrough on how to complete that analysis. This may be done by either creating a website with all of the code and data available to download or uploading a zip file containing everything needed to do an analysis.

Another more advanced option is to create an R package that can be downloaded and installed. This would allow people to use the packages within their applications and would also help with integrity issues in accessing data online.

A common complaint about R Markdown files is that the fonts are hard to read. This issue can be solved by using the "RStudio" package, automatically including a PDF version of the manuscript in a separate directory. You will need to provide the PDF document (which may be larger than the actual manuscript) where you want it to be displayed and add it to your document as usual.

People also like learning things step-by-step, so this is one reason why some journals have begun accepting R Markdown manuscripts for publication. Learning R can be time-consuming, especially when you are not familiar with the intricacies of the R language. This can make it hard to go through the code and find out exactly what that code is doing. This is because it will be much easier to read once everything is combined into one document.

R Markdown provides processes and functions that aid in easily styling documents in an automated fashion; however if you prefer manually creating R Markdown documents, manual styling of your stylesheets may still be an option.

Chapter 7: Self-Documenting Code

A good self-documenting code is one that his comments at the start of each block. The comments need to explain why the code does what it does or any unusual aspects of the code.

It's also good to document every new function in a separate file with a comment that describes what the function does and its parameters. This makes it easy for people who want to use your functions; they can open up the file and see all you need to know at a glance.

If you want self-documented code, you could even create extensive documentation outside of your program and refer readers back to that whenever possible. This is precisely what the authors of the "TLA+" language do. The authors provide extensive documentation for TLA+ on their website and include extensive comments in all source code. In addition to this, you should document what you did, why you did it, and the result any time you perform a data transformation or manipulation. This could be done in several ways. You could log an entry in a plain text file and refer to that when needed. You could generate an HTML file that always has this information available from the web browser.

Finally, if you are using a computer programming language that includes tool support for documentation generation, make sure that any code additions, deletions, or changes are appropriately documented. This will help ensure that you don't needlessly repeat yourself by repeating the same code in several places.

Good documentation is crucial; it makes your code easier to read and understand, helps other people understand what your code is doing and how to use it properly, and it's always nice if other people like you and want to work with you on projects.

It's also essential to realize that the code must be well documented if you want to create any high-quality program or solution. Self-documenting code is good, but it's not good enough. You need to go the extra mile; you need to document everything as you go to avoid gaps in understanding later on.

Comments are lines of text within a program that describe what the code is doing. A compiler processes them just like any other part of the source code, but they are not compiled into machine code and don't affect the program's operation. They exist purely to be read by human beings so that other people can understand what you are doing and correct any mistakes you've made.

Comments in a program should explain things that are not already obvious. If a statement is evident, it's probably unnecessary and should be removed. The only exception to this rule would be if the statement is concise and you want to write something else afterward on the same line or if the statement would benefit from some extra explanation.

There are lots of different types of comments in C++;

The first three comments can be written directly into the code and don't need any special tools or commands. Block comments begin with codice_1 and continue until they hit a closing bracket, while line comments start with codice_2, on the same line as what they are commenting on. Finally, C++ also supports the third kind of comment called a documentation comment. These begin with codice_3 and continue until they hit a closing codice_7; then, they are ignored by the compiler and instead processed by some tool that knows how to extract information from them to build documentation pages. A tool that can be used for this purpose is Doxygen.

If you want to use Doxygen to generate your documentation, you need to place a particular comment at the start of each relevant part of your code. This consists of two parts:

Doxygen takes this information and generates an HTML page, which can then be placed on your website or included in your program source files as needed.

There are only two rules for writing good comments; (1) make sure they are helpful and (2) make sure they are consistent. Here is an example of a statement that makes sense; this comment explains why a particular calculation is necessary. It describes how the function works and what it does but also explains why the function was written in this way rather than using some other method:
This comment is not bad, but it has a couple of flaws. The comment has been written so that it could be interpreted as saying that the calculation should be performed twice, not that it's calculating twice. It's also not complete; it doesn't explain why the value is squared before being added to the column total.

This isn't a bad comment; it explains what the code is doing and why, but there are a couple of problems with it. The first is that the comment doesn't describe the input formula_1 and formula_2 or where they came from (you have to read the function definition itself to find out). The second problem is that it is inconsistent. As you can see in this example, there are two different ways of expressing numbers; one by using digits (like) and another by using variables (such as). This cannot be very clear to other code readers, as it's not clear whether these two numbers are the same or different.

There is no definite answer to which way is best; it depends on your coding styles and what you find easier to read. There are, however, a couple of guiding rules that should be followed;

The most important thing, however, is consistency. Once you have a style that works for you, always stick with it and be sure to use it in all cases where a comment might prove helpful. Once again, an example might help explain what I'm saying here; as suggested above, line comments should always begin with codice_8 and end

with codice_9. If a line comment is longer than the single line they are commenting on, then finish with codice_7.
An even better way of making comments consistent would be to use macros. A macro is simply a piece of code that you define every time you want to comment; then, every time you want to use that comment in your code, you type the name of the macro followed by your comment, and everything compiles together automatically. This can make it very easy to ensure both the format and content of all of your comments match each other; this makes it much easier for other people to understand what each means.

Using macros does require a little more work at first, but it can make your code look very professional, and it's worth the extra effort in the long run. Macros can also be handy for more than just comments; they can also make many other short pieces of code easier to write by reducing the amount of typing you have to do.

Documentation of Plots and Visualization Code with knitr

Knitr is a package for reproducible reporting of R outputs, mainly plotting. It allows the developer to document their work and create narratives while analyzing data. These narratives incorporate code chunks that produce plots like histograms or boxplots, which showcase different aspects of visualizing data. Chunks can also be re-used to create other plots in which similar arguments apply, and they convey only modifications made. In this post, I will introduce two techniques for plotting in R and how we can construct reproducible, data-driven narratives for descriptions of the plots.
R is a very powerful but also a very complex programming language. It's not hard to learn the basics, but it's problematic to master the more advanced features like machine learning or statistics. One way to get past this barrier is by using packages that allow you to quickly and effectively make your analyses easier (and

sometimes even more effective). The R language is known for its extensive data capabilities, but it is also good with small or medium-sized data used in the social sciences.

Knitr is a package designed to make reporting your R analyses reproducible. It allows you to include chunks of R code that will be executed and produce the results you desire. You can then write your results as you would any manuscript, citing these chunks as references wherever they are used. One of the nice things about this package is that it's a pure R package (and not based on Java), making it almost compatible with every version of this excellent programming language.

Reproducible data analysis (RDA) is crucial for modern data science. The process consists of creating a framework (or template) in which data can be analyzed and results reported reproducible [1]. This is widely considered the accepted way to report your findings since it allows other people to effortlessly reproduce your analyses without re-doing them or asking you for the code. There are several tools available to help you accomplish this goal. The most popular ones are Sweave (now deprecated), knitr, and RStudio's report generator. Though they all have their pros and cons, knitr has the most advantages due to its pure R implementation. For example, Sweave doesn't support LaTeX, nor is it compatible with every R version. In addition, Sweave doesn't handle missing values very well compared to knitr.

To begin using knitr, you need to install a' knitr' package in the first place (duh). This can be accomplished through the RStudio Package Manager, the command line (like sudo install.packages("knitr")), or through a list of package repositories (like CRAN). After this step, you will have to load the library into your workspace with library(knitr)—this chunk.

It is important to note that knitr works on a chunk-by-chunk basis.

Before you produce any plot, you should load R's base graphics with library(ggplot2) because some of the parameters of ggplot objects are not saved in the document, and some output options require ggplot. For example, if you try to keep a plot using the default width and height (defined using the device), it won't appear the same when opened again if the documentation was produced a week later. It is also essential to know that R's base graphics uses points as plotting objects by default when plotting a single vector (like a vector of length one). A workaround to this issue is to convert the vector into a data frame to use rows as plotting objects.

We can create plots inside a knitr chunk with knitr::kable(...), which will produce a table with a plot on each row (as seen below). We use the "style = 'ggplot'" parameter because ggplot styles are not saved in a .html file. When this chunk is re-used again, it will have the same style as your original plot.

Another thing to remember is that some other functions used by ggplot() are not saved in the document, such as theme() or color(). This is probably the most common mistake made by beginning knitr users. When you use these functions, use maybe() to control the scales of your plots before saving them. For example, when you want to display the mean for each group, you will have to write:

M1 <- maybe(length(group) == 1L)

These two chunks create a plot of the number of cars and the proportion that are insured sold per city per year (as seen below). You can see here how knitr includes a table with all of your plots since this is a chunk that displays several plots. We want to know the number and percentage of insurance sold in each city, so we also need another column with this information.

The first thing to do is create a data frame as seen below:

Df <- mtcars %>% group_by(year) %>% summarize(proportion =

n())

This creates a dataframe with the information on the number of cars sold per city each year per insurance type. You can see that I defined an integer array with the proportion of vehicles sold in each town.

Next, we must build a new plot using ggplot() but in a table. The idea is to create a single plot but with different panels. This is done with the panel parameter of ggplot().

Using the same example, we need to know two things:

(1) the number of cars sold per city and
(2) the absolute amount of percentage of insurance sold.

The first data corresponds to the number of cars sold in each city (in each year and insurance type), so we can replace that object in df$amount with the second one, which corresponds to proportion. This can be done by adding another column called abs_amount in df$amount.

To obtain the absolute amount of insurance sold in each city, we should build a new dataframe with only one column and the number of cars sold and the insurance type information. This is easily accomplished by converting df into a tibble using tibble() from the tidyverse package (which you have to load after loading knitr). Then, you can save this information in a variable called df_abs_insurance.

The last step is to create a plot with only one panel but different elements for each panel. We do this by using ggplot's + operator (which adds new panels to an existing plot), which requires a panel vector as input. In this case, we will see the events separately for each year. To divide the data by insurance type and year, we will use two more variables: insurance_type and car_year.

Documentation of Code with the Package Readability

Most people who use R in a business environment have to distribute code or are expected to write code. Even if you are not making many c-code changes, having proper documentation is essential when distributing your work. To aid in writing clear code, you should document your code appropriately. A few simple commands within R make it easy to document your code. You can use these to create text files containing syntax and function definitions and lengthy print statements with the help() function useful for error handling and debugging.

The first documentation command is codice_2. The command allows you to include a specific code section in the text file. It will enable you to have code that was created within the R program and also code that was written in another language, such as C++ (however, not Java or Python)

Codice_3

This command can also be used to write outside comments. If you have a particularly complicated code that needs further description, it might need an entire document adjacent to the sample using codice_4. This comment should give context and explain what each sample piece is doing.

In R, there are many places for errors to be introduced. One of the best tools for debugging is the 'traceback' function, which converts the previous error into an error with information that can be used with other source code-related debugging tools. The traceback function is not only used for debugging user codes but also during the compilation of R packages.

Simple use of the traceback statement might look something like this:

Codice_5

This will show you if there is an error in your code and also where it occurred and what line contains it. However, this is located on a single line and is difficult to read if you have a lot of code. To output the traceback in a more legible format, you can use the following syntax:

Codice_6

This will output the traceback broken out into multiple lines.

Another valuable function for debugging is print() which shows a message to your screen and prints the line number at which it was called. This can be useful when debugging and executing code from an R script, as the R interpreter uses print() to run your code and show an error message.

Codice_7

This is easy enough to understand, but if you have a lot of code, this may be too much information on one line if there are many errors.

To fix this, you can use code for printing messages:

Codice_8

This will include some information about the source of the problems and show the line number at which it was executed. This is especially helpful if multiple errors happen on different lines.

There are various other ways to output variables and print this, but for now, I will recommend that you use print() as it shows the variable name in a more readable format with a line number. However, I would advise that you avoid using print() in your scripts as it makes debugging difficult because R execution is not recorded on a single line. The variables used are not always easy to read.

Exploratory data analysis often requires the transformation of your data set. In R, the codice_9 function is helpful for this purpose. It essentially allows you to modify your data and create a new object based on it. This is useful for summarizing statistics on an entire data set or creating new variables based on existing ones.

To use the function, you need to specify a few things within brackets:

Codice_10

This will then output an object that is essentially a modified version of the original one, with a few extra properties such as mean and std (standard deviation) added.

You can add extra information to your objects by adding additional properties and values. One use of this function is showing margins of error.

Codice_11

In this example, we have a new variable called 'mixed,' which we want to analyze with an estimated error margin. We want to display the margin (standard deviation) in brackets together with the expected value of the margin.

Having set up your model, you are now ready for some summary statistics on your data set using the summary() function. This allows you to make multiple figures for your data set and includes information such as mean and standard deviation, showing how many objects in each group were not used (nones).

The function uses the same brackets notation as codice_9 and allows you to create new figures based on old ones.

Codice_13

This will show a simple histogram and one of the factors in your data set with a bar chart showing how many times it occurred and what the frequency is. The other important part of summary statistics is how to spread out your values within your data set. For example, if there is only one item, this may be 0, and if there is an outlier, this could be >1.

In the following example, we will be looking at a simple data set with information about height, gender, and weight. We want to look at the variability of height, the minimum and maximum weight values, and the mean of both.

Codice_14

This shows that, on average, men are taller than women, with around a 1.6cm difference in height, while weight values are very similar. As you can see, there is a slight variation between individual heights, with some being less than 1.6cm longer than others. Still, there is no clear outlier at any point in the dataset (this could be an individual who might be different in this variable). As we can see from the bar chart, males are consistently lighter than females in weight.

R provides a simple way to do this with the codice_15 command, which shows the mean and standard deviation of data based on an entire object.

Codice_16

This will show how many of the values are above or below each value which helps see outliers within your data set. It may look like there are two small dots far to the left, but there are no deviations as most of the values lie close to each other, so every dot is close together.

This function can be used to create test datasets, and then when you want to test your statistical hypothesis by performing a t-test,

ANOVA, or regression, you can use the codice_17 function.

Codice_18

This will allow you to run a t-test that compares the mean of two groups together with other tests such as ANOVA.

The above example shows two bar charts with each group on their axis and one with both groups on the same axis, showing how close they are. This is useful if you have paired data often used for statistical tests such as for physical measurements.

Finally, you can use the summary() function with the group_by() command to create every row and column matrix. This provides a very useful way of looking at data intuitively as it gives you an overview of the entire data set based on both groups.

Chapter 8: Other R Packages for Data Visualization and Analysis

R is a robust data analysis and visualization platform rapidly becoming the go-to programming language in this data-driven world. It's easy to see why: R can be used on any operating system, has unlimited licensing possibilities, and creates high-quality graphs and charts.

With so many unique packages available for data visualization and other types of analyses in R, it can be a bit overwhelming trying to decide which one is right for you. In the following section, we'll look at some of the best packages for data visualization in R and a few of the best packages for data analyses.

D3.js is an open-source JavaScript library created by Mike Bostock to produce dynamic, interactive visualizations on the web. D3 was built upon and is still based on the idea that browsers have three vector graphics capabilities: vector graphics with raster images… and animations between them! With D3, you can create stunning interactive visuals with very little code!

The Plotly package allows you to create rich interactive charts and graphs directly in R or any other programming language, including your custom functions. It is built on top of D3.js and allows you to create interactive plots and charts with very little code!
The Venn Diagram Tool has a straightforward but powerful interface for creating and editing Venn diagrams in R. It is an open-source script that allows you to create Venn diagrams in R with a few clicks of the mouse.

The Envision package allows you to create stunning visualizations and dashboards with very little code! It is the perfect tool for anyone who wants to create beautiful reports, summaries, plots, or anything else. With Envision's open-source nature and ease of use, you can customize the package to suit your style!

This custom-built environment brings together multiple tools into one convenient package. You'll get a 3D interface for creating and editing geographic data, aerial data, and satellite imagery maps. In this environment, you'll be able to import your custom shapes and associated legends from R or a vector/image file.

The CartoDbR package allows you to create interactive maps in R without leaving the comfort of your computer! This package creates live visualizations that update as you change data or add new features. It is effortless to use as well!

The d3heatmap package creates interactive maps using heatmap() in the HTML5 canvas element. Because it does not require Flash or other plugins, this is an excellent way to keep data graphics up-to-date for web use.

The GISTerm package creates interactive charts in the R console. Because it does not require Flash or other plugins, this is an excellent way to keep data graphics up-to-date for web use.

The IqR package allows you to create interactive maps in R without leaving the comfort of your computer! This package creates live visualizations that update as you change data or add new features. It is effortless to use as well.

The MAGick image manipulation and visualization library handles nearly all types of image manipulation, including resizing, rotating, converting to grayscale, color conversion and blending, scaling, and perspective transformations. MAGick also supports many file formats, including JPEG, PNG, and GIF.

The MASS package allows you to create interactive maps in R without having to leave the comfort of your computer! This package creates live visualizations that update as you change data or add new features. It is straightforward to use as well!

The Mapnik package allows you to create interactive maps in R without having to leave the comfort of your computer! This package creates live visualizations that update as you change data or add new features. It is very easy to use as well!

The mapproj package allows you to create interactive maps in R without leaving the comfort of your computer! This package creates live visualizations that update as you change data or add new features. It is very easy to use as well!

The maptools package allows you to create interactive maps in R without leaving the comfort of your computer! This package creates live visualizations that update as you change data or add new features. It is very easy to use as well!

The RColorBrewer package allows you to create interactive maps in R without leaving the comfort of your computer! This package creates live visualizations that update as you change data or add new features. It is very easy to use as well!

RStudio lets you build shiny applications and websites with R, a free programming language for statistical computing and graphics. With RStudio, you will be able to connect to any relational database, big or small.

Shiny Applications is a web application that allows you to build interactive web applications with R in a simple and user-friendly environment.

shinyBS allows you to build interactive graphics and replot them as others request them with minimal overhead. This is ideal for presentations, reports, and dashboards where the same data (or subset) is needed repeatedly. The best part? Even Shiny newbies can make use of shinyBS!

A Shiny App Template lets you export your app menu information from RStudio so that it can be embedded into another webpage. It even includes a title, description, and critical component images!

Introduction to RStudio and Shiny Apps in R

After joining the language of R, Statistics and Data Science becomes a lot more fun because it focuses on the use of data visualization. In order to get a grasp on what R is capable of and how you can leverage its ability to visualize data, we have compiled a list of the most popular R packages for graphics.

"R" stands for "Racket", which makes sense if you think about it – in this language, one can easily work efficiently with mathematical equations and statistical analysis. After all, this is the world's most widely used programming language.

In "R", RStudio is a user-friendly IDE that allows you to work with R in an interactive environment. Depending on the platform you are using, "RStudio", "Shiny" or "Graphic" packages can be integrated in your code. It provides all the necessary functionality for developing, testing, and debugging your code. You can get started right away with R, a programming language that is popular among statisticians and data scientists.

Software developers can write code for their product quickly with minimal errors because their language caters to the long-time analyses required by certain fields of science. It works on multiple platforms and enables you to build applications that can be used by non-programmers.

R is a very powerful language, particularly when it comes to analyzing data. Rstudio is the most popular IDE for creating apps in R. It has a lot of libraries that make the process of creating R data visualization applications much faster and easier. In this article, we will look at what it takes to create interactive graphics with the help of Shiny in Rstudio.

RStudio is an integrated development environment (IDE) for R, which makes developing applications easy for statisticians and data scientists. It supports various programming languages, including Python, Java, R, and more.

R Studio makes it very easy to use R by organizing the code in a single document. It also has a code completion feature, which comes in handy when you're using data frames and other structures. In addition to that, there are several other features that make it an ideal choice for both new and experienced users.

Shiny is an open-source web application framework for R that makes it possible to build interactive applications for the web. It uses reactive programming and allows users to create well-designed apps without having to write HTML or CSS code. The main benefit of Shiny is that apps can be tailored to fit your specific needs and also used to create dashboards.

The code for a complete application is stored in a single file, which makes it easy to maintain your code. It also integrates perfectly with databases like MongoDB, MySQL, PostgreSQL and more. You can use R Markdown documents or HTML files in the development of your application.

"Graphic" is a collection of various graphics functions which can be used to create graphics in R. The functions include line plot, bar chart, pie chart, histogram etc. It provides an easy way to generate visual output for statistical computing languages like Python or R. Graphics for "Graphic" is provided by the R graphics system.

Shiny integrates very well with R, making it possible to use it for building interactive apps for the web. It has been created and maintained by the team at hackR, a center that provides open source software for data science, machine learning, and data visualization. The focus of this framework is to make it easier for developers to create compelling data visualizations.

The aim of this package is to develop a Shiny application in R that makes it easy to visualize data generated by built-in functions in R. It has several features for producing charts, including pixelwise and hexbit approximation.

This package is intended for data visualization in R and can be used to create interactive visualizations for the web. It supports a number of useful functions including heatmap and scatterplot.

The aim of these packages is to provide easy-to-use tools for creating R programs that can be used to display data and make inferences about the data. These graphics packages are designed specifically for web applications, which makes them superior when compared to other proprietary systems.

Using R, Statisticians and Data scientists can make their quantitative analyses much easier and faster by integrating them with ease into a visual representation at the same time.

The most challenging aspect of using R as a data analysis tool is the amount of time it would take to visualize big sets of data. A lot of such applications may simply not be possible otherwise.

By using R, you can produce beautiful graphics by just including certain functions in your code. These graphs are produced rapidly, which allows you to detect any possible issues and make changes accordingly. The process allows you to streamline your analysis and make sure that the final output is what you expected it to be.

R is especially useful when it comes to analyzing the data with hundreds or thousands of variables attached to various entities in a dataset. Data visualization tools can help you to easily detect patterns that have been present in the data but which have not been discovered yet.

You can carry out a number of statistical computations, including linear and logistic regression, clustering, and more with R. The process is very quick and easy to perform, allowing you to get the results quickly in your hands.

Using R Studio IDE combined with a variety of graphics packages makes it easy for you to do basic data analysis, time series analysis, and several other tasks that are relevant to statisticians and scientists.

RStudio IDE enables developers to create web-based applications using R language as the front-end programming language. You can create interactive web applications which are easy for non-programmers to use.

Rstudio IDE is designed to support several programming languages, including Python and R, making it a very powerful tool that enables you to develop and test your code rapidly. Python is a powerful scripting language that can be used to create graphical interfaces. It is easy to use and well suited to various application development tasks.

RStudio IDE also supports a number of programming languages, including Python, R, Ruby JQuery, and more. This makes both the development process as well as the testing process a lot faster and easier.

You can create your application using several programming languages by using Rstudio IDE. This makes it much easier for you to integrate several frameworks into your apps for developing comprehensive solutions for complex problems.

Rstudio IDE comes with libraries that help you to quickly develop web-based applications in R language. These libraries are very useful in helping you create interactive data visualizations, which are easy for non-programmers to understand as well as use.

This package provides the necessary code to run a web-based data visualization application. It allows you to develop visualizations that show data in different ways and uses several animation techniques to generate impressive results.

The main aim of this package is to assist data analysts and statisticians with creating visualizations of their own data, which is easy for non-data scientists to understand as well as use. Using this pack, you can make sure that the final output matches your expectations.

This example shows how a simple scatterplot can be used with the core function in R. The code is very easy to understand and is entirely written in R. This can be done without any additional libraries or packages.

This open-source package was developed to provide interactive visualizations of data. It allows you to animate various types of data, by providing a lot of useful features that are compatible with many programming languages available in R.

Rstudio IDE allows developers to create web-based applications using the R language as the main front-end programming language. You can develop visualizations that display different kinds of data, including charts & graphs and other kinds of information that are relevant to statistics and data analysis.

This package is designed for developers who want an effortless way to create interactive visualizations for the web. This pack is especially useful when it comes to creating maps, tree maps, and heatmaps.

This package was designed to be a simple and easy-to-use data visualization module for R. It has several useful features, including the ability to use different layouts for arranging information in a simple way.

This package allows you to visualize data that is stored in SQL databases in the form of tables, which makes it very useful for data analysts and statisticians who are dealing with this kind of information in their everyday professional lives.

Using Rstudio IDE, you can create web-based applications using R language as the main front-end programming language. You can develop interactive map visualizations that are compatible with big sets of geographical information. RStudio IDE makes it easy for non-programmers to create interactive data visualizations using this tool.

Rstudio IDE enables developers to create web-based applications that are based on R language. This makes it possible to develop interactive visualizations that will help you to present your data in a more effective and easier way.

Rstudio IDE is an open source community project which allows you to develop interactive data visualizations using various techniques and libraries, including HTML5 and JavaScript in order to do so.

This package uses the R language as the main front-end programming language for creating a web-based application for data visualization purposes.

D3.js for Web Graphic on a Server Machine

D3 is a JavaScript library that is used to make data-driven documents, and it's easy to use CSS which allows your web graphics or web pages with D3. The D3 projects is divided into three parts: Data visualization on the server machine, data visualization on the client machines via d3.js html5 canvas element, and mobile devices / desktop applications using a WebWorker process with Electron's BrowserWindow as parent process. D3 can be used as a visual data representation and data form of statistical analysis that are based on the node object in the graph. For example, you can visualize the data to visualize a line chart, bar chart, scatter plot, and so on. The library is developed in JavaScript, which uses scenes to produce graphics, and has been widely used in different areas such as information visualization, scientific computing, and so on.

D3 is divided into two major parts: the core of D3 (d3.js) and modules (d3-scale). Each module allows for some functionality to be added to D3. For example, d3-scale adds functionality for scales and axis annotations.

Supports the creation of SVG, which is based on an XML format.

After the data is passed to the D3 library, it is converted into a visual representation by using the D3 library. D3 data supports many different types of charts, such as bar charts (bar), line charts (line), scatter plots (scatter), and so on. The final picture can be stored in a variety of transparency formats, such as PNG and SVG.

You can create your own data visualization design using D3 by using HTML elements to create a graph. You can make this graph with D3.js in JavaScript, or export it as SVG on the server side and display it on the web page.

The main challenge is to support the creation of SVG files and serving them in the right way; experience has shown that creating SVG images directly from JavaScript is not a good idea. Although this allows you to do some basic file formats (e.g., PNG), its methods of handling images may result in scaling images, which is far from ideal when attempting to provide high-quality graphics to viewers on different platforms (phone, tablet, and desktop).

The solution is to create SVG files on the server side, then simply add the SVG images to the web page. Of course, some data visualization libraries provide better support for this than others. In particular, if you are using Mike Bostock's D3 library, which is the most widespread one and follows a modular approach, there are even modules that can be added to the core of d3.js to support server-side image generation in various image formats (e.g., PNG). HTML5 canvas element also helps with this approach when used together with d3.js via data-driven rendering of graphics as well as providing tools for reading and writing images to disk for further use.

The advantages in this case is that the SVG images are already cached by the browser, but the downside is that data visualization can only be done on the client side – there is no server-side support for server-side image generation. The D3 library does not provide a means of reading and writing data from/to disk on its own. However, it can work together with other libraries such as HTML5 canvas. R, Excel, and Matlab can be used to create charts in SVG, which can later be served from server to client using XMLHttpRequest.

In this case, you would first create a chart (e.g., bar chart) using JavaScript. You would then use the D3.js library to create an SVG file from the chart. This SVG can be served from the server and used to render a bar chart on the client side with either HTML5 canvas or D3.js.

Although this is not an ideal solution, it is well supported – provided you are using Mike Bostock's D3 library, which provides a number of modules that will help you in creating SVG charts on the server side and serving it in a proper manner. One of these modules is ServerSideImageGenerator, which uses Apache Cordova to create PNG images and allows for caching such images so that they can be loaded much faster if you need them later.

The advantages in this case is the ability to have a version of the chart that is generated on the server side and can be used for rendering on the client side via HTML5 canvas or d3.js. The main disadvantage is that data visualization can only be done on the client side – there is no server-side support for generating charts.

HTML5 Canvas and necessary JavaScript APIs on client machines allow you to load web pages that are visualized on a Canvas element, similar to what was used in Flash-based games in yesteryears.

On the client side, you can load the page that was created on the server and render the data visualization on the Canvas element.

The advantages in this case are that it's possible to render it in real-time on a mobile device and desktop computer. The main disadvantage is that data visualization can only be done on the client side — there is no server-side support for generating charts.

Information graphics and visualizations has had a very long tradition and contributed to many disciplines of science and culture, like astronomy, pedagogy, media analysis etc. However, information graphics is still behind a wall of misunderstandings/misunderstandings and lack of guidelines/best practices. Most projects in the fields of information visualization are not necessarily aligned with the best practices listed below because most of them are still in their early stage of evolution. The aim is to raise awareness and discuss about the issues, conclusions, and best practices based on real-life examples.

Graphic design is a method used to present information in a way that it can be more easily understood and more effectively used. The graphic designer has to work with big data, limited time, and resources. Graphic design has evolved to become a form of communicating ideas and needs through visual means. It is done by combining the visual elements of line, shape, color, and space with text to communicate messages via images.

Visual communication is an effective way of communicating a message because the brain processes visual information faster than text or audio communications. Visual elements like line, color, and shape are ideal tools for communicating messages because they stimulate the brain more than words do.

The information graphic designer has to deal with big data, and limited time and resources to deliver the message without losing the integrity of the message. Relationships between objects or concepts have to be structured so that they are easily understandable by anyone. The message must be effectively communicated in a way that is understood quickly.

In information graphics, the purpose of designing a graphic is to communicate a concept or idea clearly to an audience who may not have any prior knowledge or experience of the subject matter. The emphasis is on effective communication rather than visual art, although there is overlap between information graphics and visual design (or more specifically within what is called infographics: visualization techniques + an added layer of textual information).

Like with any other design discipline, information graphics follow the fundamental principles of graphic design. Information graphics uses a set of communication principles in which there is a balance between design, data, and narrative elements. The content, as well as the visual presentation, has to be consistent. Information graphics are also made in a way that allows them to be understood by various levels of readers (i.e. from general readers to experts). The amount of text per unit area should also be carefully considered to ensure that it can be easily read by the audience and is not too much or little information on the page or the visualization (the optimum range is between 2% and 9% of text per image area). The message should be strongly communicated to the audience in a way that they will take time to re-read the information.

The best way to learn about visualization and information graphics is to practice visualizing your data. Visual data can be used as a tool to communicate with an audience by using the specific characteristics of visualization, such as color, shape, size, density, etc.

Visual data also allows for more effective and efficient communication as compared to traditional ways of presenting data. Creating visualizations is a great learning experience that can be applied in any other graphics design field.

One of the most important considerations when designing an information graphic is to compare the advantages and disadvantages of different visualization methods. It is important to choose those that will allow you to communicate your message in the best possible way.

For example, infographics are used most often when it comes to communicating scientific information (i.e. top-10 lists, etc.). Another example of an information graphic is a wireframe diagram. It is commonly used to visually represent the structure and hierarchy of a product or system. Network diagrams and flowcharts are often used to visualize business processes, while financial statements are visualized on bar charts.

The main goal of an information graphic is to effectively communicate information by using visual elements to create understanding through visual perception. It also gives an opportunity to use new visualization techniques such as mapping and animations (i.e. GIFs).

Depending on how complicated the data is that it has to present, there are different approaches to representing data (i.e. simple bar charts vs complex network diagrams).

Color and shape are the most common visual elements in information graphics.

Color provides an easy way to convey meaning and shape gives a shape to the information presented.

The type of information that is being communicated also has an influence on the visual elements that are used. For example, if it is a scientific chart, then it will probably use a lot of colors, drawn diagrams, and bar graphs, while in case of business, this may be more similar to text and Excel spreadsheets. It must be noted, though, that there should be some appropriate core visual elements for each type of message.

Visual data can be used as a tool to communicate ideas or concepts with different audiences. Where other forms of data are dry, visual data can tell stories or provide metaphors for people without having them directly experience the data itself. Visual data is a great tool to understand the data and how it can be used by various users without having to actually see it.

An example of how visual data can be used like this would be the visualization of crime rates using heat maps. Heat maps are commonly used to show the distribution of crimes over time and space. They can also use other forms of visual data, such as line graphs, stacked bar charts, etc., in order to depict the same information in an appropriate way.

Conclusion

Research data is hard to process and turn into meaningful insights, which is why we created a new R package called RVisualize. This package provides an intuitive interface for visualizing data in a convincing manner without the need for any code or experience in graphics or programming.

RVisualize provides three types of graphs: bar charts, line charts, and scatter plots with smoothed curves. The user can select which type of graph they want to display based on the number of observations they have, as well as how much error they want to compensate for. The convenience factor makes it easy to visualize and communicate complex research output quickly. There are also other useful visualizations, including parallel coordinates and radial-bar plots.

The package was developed using shiny, a web application framework for R. The plots are rendered using the Highcharts JavaScript library. The current version of the package is hosted on Github, where users can download it for free for various types of research projects involving data and statistics.

In closing, RVisualize provides an intuitive way to create novel data visualization designs in R and lets you create graphics that are similar to those made in MATLAB or Python. Feel free to use this package any time you are working with research data that you want to communicate in an effective manner. We hope that you find it as useful as we do. If you do, please share it with your friends.

Researchers have been using R to visualize data for a long time now. In the beginning, R users would take plain text datasets or other types of files, save them as comma-separated values (CSV) files and then import them into R. The user would then use basic tools within R to create plots from these data sets. Visualization packages like lattice and ggplot2 came along and improved upon this process by making it easier for the user to create more specific types of graphs in a simpler way. These packages also provide a wide range of different plots to choose from. However, these packages do not allow the user to create interactive visualizations. In order to accomplish this, users have to write R code within the interactive R console or use base graphics functions like plot() or lines().

The goal of this new data visualization package is to let the user create excellent looking graphs that can be shared online and embedded in various types of documents seamlessly. The end result is a graph that looks as if it were created in MATLAB or Python. The package is called RVisualize, and it will be released on CRAN soon and made freely available for all users interested in using it for research work involving data visualizations.

The package was developed using the shiny web application framework for R. RVisualize uses the Highcharts JavaScript library to render the graphs and comes with a large number of different types of graphs to choose from.

What's next?

The package is still in development, and additional features will be implemented over the next few months. We are also doing research to improve the performance of the package and are currently running tests for determining which types of plots are best suited for each specific type of data. PLOS ONE recently announced that they would begin requiring authors to submit figures and tables as supplemental material. This supports our theory that interactive visualizations have an increasing range of applications in the scientific community.

Currently, RVisualize provides three different types of plots: scatter plots with smoothed curves, line charts and bar charts. In the future, we plan to add support for many other types of graphs, such as parallel coordinates plots, histograms, and boxplots.

We hope that you find R-Visualize useful and will be a good replacement for plain text files, MATLAB, and Python within your research work involving data visualizations. If you do, please share it with your friends.

There are many R visualization packages on CRAN, and most of them are great. However, there is currently only one package that provides the user with a GUI that allows them to create different types of graphs in a simpler manner than base graphics functions. The Shiny package makes it possible to create interactive visualizations in the R console with code like runGist(g) or runApp(myApp). It is currently the most popular visualization tool in the R community.

The goal of this new data visualization package is to let users create excellent-looking graphs that can be shared online and embedded in various types of documents seamlessly. The end result is a graph that looks as if it were created in MATLAB or Python. The package is called RVisualize, and it will be released on CRAN soon and made freely available for all users interested in using it for research work involving data visualizations.

www.ingramcontent.com/pod-product-compliance
Lightning Source LLC
Chambersburg PA
CBHW060421220526
45465CB00008B/2974